GREAT
BRITISH
LOSERS

GREAT BRITISH LOSERS

Heroic Failures and Brazen Bunglers

GORDON KERR

First published in the United Kingdom in 2011 by:
Old Street Publishing Ltd,
Trebinshun House, Brecon LD3 7PX
www.oldstreetpublishing.co.uk

ISBN-13: 978-1-905847-56-3

Copyright in the text © Gordon Kerr
Copyright in the illustrations © James Nunn

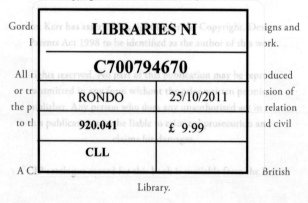
Gordon Kerr has asserted his right under the Copyright, Designs and Patents Act 1998 to be identified as the author of this work.

All rights reserved. No part of this publication may be reproduced or transmitted in any form or without the prior written permission of the publisher. Any person who does any unauthorised act in relation to this publication may be liable to criminal prosecution and civil claims for damages.

A CIP catalogue record for this book is available from the British Library.

This book is sold subject to the condition that it shall not, by way of trade or otherwise, be lent, re-sold, hired out, or otherwise circulated without the publisher's prior consent, in any form or binding or cover other than that in which it is published and without a similar condition including this condition being imposed on the subsequent purchaser.

10 9 8 7 6 5 4 3 2 1

'You don't win silver. You lose gold'

NIKE ADVERT

'Part of me suspects that I'm a loser, and the other part of me thinks I'm God Almighty'

JOHN LENNON

LIST OF LOSERS

Introduction

Why do the British love losers? In fact, not only love them, but celebrate them, reward them, garland them with prizes, and write books about them? Even the wars and battles we have lost somehow end up being celebrated, often more than our great victories.

Relentless victory is boring. Life is much more fun if you don't know who's going to win. (Of course, if you support certain football teams – Scotland for example – you usually do know who's going to win. The other side.)

To the untrained eye, some of the losers in this book look very much like winners. They had all the trappings of success. But they missed out on their life's ambition, or made just one fatal error – the cock-up that everyone remembers. It might seem unfair that so many of those we denounce as 'losers' were or are far more successful than most of us will ever be – talented and dedicated individuals, *almost* at the peak of their profession, or with a string of victories to their name.

But if these stories tell us anything, it's that life isn't fair. Stuff (a.k.a. 'shit') happens. And let's face it, we're all losers at some point or other in our lives. Everyone, great or small, is capable of turning glorious victory into embarrassing defeat. In this book I celebrate some of our nation's best and noblest failures. Naturally, I have also taken the opportunity to haul some absolute rotters over the coals.

Yet there is greatness in many of these losers – often, perhaps, a very British kind of greatness.

Gordon Kerr, September 2011

Caractacus:
The Man Who Lost Britain

When Caractacus, king of the Catevallauni, conquered a rival tribe, the Atrebates, their leader Verica went scurrying off for help to the Roman emperor Claudius. In 43 AD the mighty Rome launched an invasion of this cold, wet island on the edge of the known world. The somewhat predictable result was Britain's centuries-long submission to the Roman Empire.

Caractacus and his brother Togodumnus led guerrilla attacks against the invaders, but in two critical battles on the rivers Medway and Thames, Togodumnus lost his life, and the Catevallauni their territories.

Caractacus gamely carried on the fight, retreating to the west and fighting for nine years from Wales against Scapula, the Roman Governor of Britain. But in 51 AD, out-manoeuvred by the Romans, Caractacus lost for the last time. His wife and his remaining brothers were captured, but Caractacus himself escaped, this time heading north to the lands of the Brigantes, in modern Yorkshire. But in a display of the legendary Yorkshire hospitality, the Brigantine queen Cartimandua welcomed him by putting him in chains and handing him over to the Romans, whose friendship she was keen to cultivate.

As was traditional for captured foreign kings and queens, Caractacus was sent to Rome to be paraded before the people prior to his execution. However, he was allowed to make a final speech to the Roman Senate, during which he praised Rome for her glorious victory over the Britons. He must have laid it on pretty thick, because he was handed a pardon and allowed to live out his days in Rome.

Meanwhile, the land he had fought for stayed in Roman hands until the fifth century AD. Then came the Angles, Saxons, Jutes, Normans...

99

Michael Fish:
Hurricane? What hurricane?

On the night of 15 October 1987, Michael Fish MBE told the nation that a woman had rung in to say that she'd heard there was a hurricane on the way.

'Well, don't worry,' Fish continued in his reassuringly avuncular manner. 'There isn't.' He went on to forecast 'sea breezes' and a 'showery airflow' – whatever that is.

A few hours later the worst storm to hit England since the Great Storm of 1703 blew in from the Atlantic, ravaging the country with 120mph winds, ripping up 300 miles of power cables, plunging a quarter of the country's inhabitants into darkness, tearing trees from the ground and blocking more than 200 roads. At least 18 people died that night as a result of the storm, and the next day all rail traffic in southern England was halted.

A spokesman for Michael Fish said, 'It's really all a question of detail.' It wasn't a hurricane, you see, just an intense North Atlantic depression...

Robert Coates:
The Worst Actor in the World

Robert 'Romeo' Coates was such a bad actor that police had to stand guard at his performances to prevent things getting out of hand.

Born in Antigua in 1772 to a wealthy sugar plantation owner, Coates inherited the estate when his father died in 1807, but soon moved to Britain, where he set up home in Bath. A Major Pryse Lockhart Gordon gave him his entrée to the theatre, having heard him recite passages from Shakespeare over breakfast in the hotel where they were both staying. Gordon noted that Coates did not always stick entirely to the text as written by the Bard, but nevertheless found his tone striking and offered to introduce him to the manager of the local Theatre Royal. In 1809, having bribed the theatre's manager, Coates stepped onto an English stage for the first time, to perform in *Romeo and Juliet*. Such was the audience's derision for Coates' performance, however, that the play failed to make it to its tragic denouement.

Thus was the most misguided of theatrical careers launched. That it continued for so long could only have been the result of the wholesale bribery of theatre managers all over Britain.

Coates' performances were notoriously calamitous. He frequently forgot his lines, and on a whim would invent entire new scenes and bits of dialogue, throwing his fellow actors into confusion as they tried to keep up. If he particularly liked a scene, he would simply repeat it. Death scenes were his favourite, and he often died onstage three or four times in a single night – in every sense of the word.

On one occasion when Coates was playing Romeo – clad in a costume of his own design that consisted of a sequinned cloak, red pantaloons, a huge cravat and a plumed hat – he left the stage, returned with a crowbar and unaccountably began to pry open the Capulet tomb. Meanwhile the actress playing Juliet clung to a nearby pillar, looking on in horror, too traumatised to leave the stage. Needless to say, as time went on, it became increasingly difficult to find an actress willing to play Juliet to his eccentric Romeo.

Another time he dropped a diamond buckle while making his exit from the stage and spent some considerable time crawling around on all fours looking for it, while the other actors did their best to carry on with the performance.

Wittingly or otherwise, Coates left audiences rolling in the aisles wherever he went, and his infamy soon spread throughout Britain. None other than the Prince Regent attended one performance in London. When he played Lothario in *The Fair Penitent* at London's Haymarket Theatre, there was a near riot when thousands of people, eager to see for themselves whether Coates was as bad as they had heard, had to be turned away from the theatre. In Richmond, several audience members are said to have required medical attention, having injured themselves laughing. Yet Coates remained constant in his belief that he was the best actor in Britain.

His offstage persona was no less flamboyant. A nineteenth-century version of Liberace, he wore huge fur coats even at the height of summer, and would emerge from his custom-built carriage, emblazoned with the heraldic device of a crowing cock, to dazzle onlookers with the diamonds that festooned his clothes and buckles.

Sadly neither fame nor fortune lasted. When his star eventually waned, he moved to Boulogne in France, married and had children, before later returning to live in London.

His final bow was as ignominious as all the rest. Robert Coates, the worst actor in history, was run over by a Hansom Cab in 1848. For once, he didn't get up and die all over again...

'Is there any beginning to your talents?'

CLIVE ANDERSON, TELEVISION PRESENTER,

TO JEFFREY ARCHER

WEST END FLOPS

West End shows are a gamble. A star-studded production that has wowed the provinces can still fall flatter than a novice chef's soufflé when it reaches the capital. For every surprise success, a dozen money-haemorrhaging failures are swept out of the theatre before the understudy has even had time to grease the stairs. Here are a few of the most egregious flops.

The Nondescript

This musical farce, put on at Covent Garden in the early 19th century and with an effeminate haberdasher named Billy Smirker as its hero, was so bad that it failed to finish a single performance. The booing that greeted the end of Act One was so venomous that the actors had fled the theatre before the curtain went up for Act Two.

Jeeves: The Musical

Even the greats can suffer the ignominy of early doors. Andrew Lloyd-Webber and Alan Ayckbourn combined their not inconsiderable talents to create the musical *Jeeves*, based on the novels of P.G. Wodehouse. As Wodehouse himself might have put it, the show laid an instantaneous egg, staggering through just 38 performances between 22nd April 1975 and 24th May 1975 at Her Majesty's Theatre in London, before the curtain came down for the last time, gifting Lloyd-Webber his only flop. (Perhaps its time had not come, since in 1996 Lloyd-Webber revived it in a rewritten version, *By Jeeves*, which was a great success in London before transferring to Broadway in 2001.)

Money To Burn

Written by actor Daniel Abineri of the TV sitcom *Bless Me, Father*, and starring someone from *Hi-De-Hi* and a Fame Academy loser, *Money To Burn* was a musical about a badly behaved aristocrat with a penchant for being spanked. It lasted just two nights, in October 2003. 'Not even bad enough to be good,' opined the *Daily Telegraph*, while the *Daily Mail* described it as 'a shocker of a show', adding that Abineri's 'lyrics and libretto are as dim as his chances of a box office success'.

Oscar Wilde: The Musical

Staged at the Shaw Theatre in October 2004 to commemorate the 150th anniversary of the eponymous hero's birth, *Oscar Wilde: The Musical* was cancelled after just one performance and universally vitriolic reviews. One theatre critic complained that it was 'hard to feel anything other than incredulous contempt' for the show. Meanwhile, commenting on technical problems, the *Guardian* put the boot in: 'the sound system is being affected by the hefty rumbling of Oscar Wilde turning in his grave.' The much-derided libretto, written in rhyming couplets, was penned by former Radio One DJ Mike Read, whose famous refusal, on moral grounds, to play Frankie Goes To Hollywood's *Relax* might have suggested that he was not the ideal candidate to dramatize the life of the notorious libertine Wilde.

The Far Pavilions

When the musical version of M.M. Kaye's epic 1978 bestseller about the Raj, *The Far Pavilions*, opened at London's Shaftesbury Theatre in April 2005, it was obvious pretty quickly that it was tanking. So badly, in fact, that the producer, Michael E. Ward, announced that he would refund the audience's money at the interval if they were not enjoying the show. Ward was invited onto BBC Two's *Newsnight*, where Jeremy Paxman did not disappoint, welcoming him with the question: 'Let's face it, it's crap, isn't it?'

The Man In the Iron Mask

This disastrous 2005 musical only lasted three performances, after receiving one of the most savage critical beatings ever suffered by a work for the stage. Written by Professor John Robinson, a former aerospace engineer, it starred Sheila Ferguson, erstwhile member of the girl singing group The Three Degrees, much loved by Prince Charles. It told the story of the unknown man who was secretly put into a mask and imprisoned in 17th-century France under Louis XIV. The *Daily Telegraph* suggested that the cast performed 'as if they have been on a prolonged Mogadon bender'. Leading man Robert Fardell was memorably described in the *Guardian* as looking like 'Hannibal Lecter crossed with a Teletubby'; the *Evening Standard* disagreed, opining that he looked more like 'a charred parrot'.

97

John Smith:
Wig-maker and Highwayman

John Smith was bad from the beginning, and going to sea failed to improve him. By 1704, aged 23, he was living in London and working in the wig trade, where he got to know a fellow wig-maker with premises in Chancery Lane. There was plenty of money in wigs – in those days they were *de rigueur* at every level of society, for both men and women – but Smith and his friend felt the need to augment their income. They decided to become highwaymen.

The two wig-makers-slash-highwaymen launched their new careers on Sunday 29 October in Paddington, then a village on the outskirts of London, situated uncomfortably close to the gallows at Tyburn. So close, in fact, that as they waited Smith lost his nerve and considered abandoning the venture. His associate talked him out of it, and the pair eventually held up the hapless William Birch, stealing his grey mare from under him.

The next day Smith went solo, robbing three stagecoaches near Epping Forest. Two days later he held up another three stagecoaches and a Hackney carriage on Hounslow Heath. On the following Saturday, he robbed three stagecoaches near St. Albans. The week's efforts netted him twenty pounds – around £1,500 in today's money.

The next Monday, on Finchley Common, he robbed a coach owned by Thomas Woodcock, pocketing four guineas, two keys and a silk purse. Unfortunately for Smith, a man rode past shortly after the robbery, and took off in pursuit. Smith headed for a nearby wood, where he went to ground, but his grey mare was soon found tied to a bush. A huntsman who had joined in the chase then spotted Smith cowering in the undergrowth and approached him, wielding a loaded blunderbuss. The wig-maker chose to give himself up rather than be ventilated with lead shot.

Poor John Smith, a highwayman for just over a week, was tried and found guilty of robbery. On 20 December 1704 he paid a second visit to Tyburn, this time to be hanged.

96

Jemini: Nul Points

Britain's Eurovision experience has been, to say the very least, chequered. True, British entries have won five times in the competition's 55-year history, the last being in 1997, courtesy of adopted American band Katrina and the Waves. But since then we've floundered badly, with Jessica Garlick, third in 2002, providing the only bright spot in recent years.

The national nadir, at least in Eurovision terms, came in 2003 when Jemini, comprising Liverpool singers Chris Cromby and Gemma Abbey, sang the execrable *Cry Baby*. With this they achieved the legendary *nul points*, finishing twenty-sixth out of twenty-six (as all Eurovision lovers know, this is traditionally the prerogative of the Norwegian entry). Soon after, Abbey could be found working in a car showroom and Cromby in a clothes shop.

On the night Jemini claimed that they were unable to hear their backing track, and there were dark mutterings of backstage sabotage. Others attribute their ignominy to international politics. Terry Wogan, the doyen of Eurovision commentary, had warned the group before the contest that Britain's involvement in the invasion of Iraq would scupper their chances.

In recent years the contest has been more blighted than ever by political voting, with Greece voting for Cyprus, former Soviet bloc countries voting for whomever they happen to be friendly with at the time, and so on. And, of course, nobody voting for the British.

BRITAIN'S EUROVISION FAILURES IN ASCENDING ORDER

Year	Act	Title	Position	Points
2003	Jemini	*Cry Baby*	26th	0*
2010	Josh Dubovie	*That Sounds Good To Me*	25th	7*
2008	Andy Abraham	*Even If*	25th	14*
2007	Scooch	*Flying the Flag (For You)*	23rd	19
2005	Javine	*Touch My Fire*	22nd	18
2006	Daz Sampson	*Teenage Life*	19th	25
2004	James Fox	*Hold On To Our Love*	16th	29
2000	Nicki French	*Don't Play That Song Again*	16th	28
2001	Lindsay Dracass	*No Dream Impossible*	15th	28
1987	Rikki	*Only The Light*	13th	47
1999	Precious	*Say It Again*	12th	38
1978	Coco	*The Bad Old Days*	11th	61
1994	Frances Ruffelle	*We Will be Free (Lonely Symphony)*	10th	63
1995	Love City Groove	*Love City Groove*	10th	76
1991	Samantha Janus	*A Message To Your Heart*	10th	47
1966	Kenneth McKellar	*A Man Without Love*	9th	8

1996	Gina G	*Ooh Ah…Just A Little Bit*	8th	77
1986	Ryder	*Runner In the Night*	7th	72
1984	Belle & The Devotions	*Love Games*	7th	63
1979	Black Lace	*Mary Anne*	7th	73
1982	Bardo	*One Step Further*	7th	76
1957	Patricia Bredin	*All*	7th **	6
1990	Emma	*Give a Little Love Back to the World*	6th	87
1983	Sweet Dreams	*I'm Never Giving Up*	6th	79
2011	Blue	*I Can*	5th	100
2009	Jade Ewen	*It's My Time*	5th	173
1985	Vikki	*Love Is*	4th	100
1971	Clodagh Rodgers	*Jack In The Box*	4th	98
1974	Olivia Newton John	*Long Live Love*	4th	14
1963	Ronnie Carroll	*Say Wonderful Things*	4th	28
1962	Ronnie Carroll	*Ring-A-Ding Girl*	4th	10
2002	Jessica Garlick	*Come Back*	3rd	111
1980	Prima Donna	*Love Enough For Two*	3rd	106
1973	Cliff Richard	*Power To All Our Friends*	3rd	123
1998	Imaani	*Where Are You*	2nd	166
1993	Sonia	*Better the Devil You Know*	2nd	164
1992	Michael Ball	*One Step Out of Time*	2nd	139
1989	Live Report	*Why Do I Always Get It Wrong?*	2nd	130
1988	Scott Fitzgerald	*Go*	2nd	136

1977	Lynsey De Paul & Mike Moran	*Rock Bottom*	2nd	121
1975	The Shadows	*Let Me Be the One*	2nd	138
1972	The New Seekers	*Beg Steal Or Borrow*	2nd	114
1970	Mary Hopkin	*Knock Knock Who's? There*	2nd	26
1968	Cliff Richard	*Congratulations*	2nd	28
1965	Kathy Kirby	*I Belong*	2nd	26
1964	Matt Monro	*I Love The Little Things*	2nd	17
1961	The Allisons	*Are You Sure*	2nd	24
1960	Bryan Johnson	*Looking High High High*	2nd	25
1959	Pearl Carr & Teddy Johnson	*Little Birdie*	2nd	16

(The United Kingdom did not enter the contest in 1958)
* Last place
** Of 10 entrants

95

Edward Hyde, 3rd Earl of Clarendon: Cross-dressing Governor of New York

One night in the early 1700s, a New York constable arrested a woman he believed to be a prostitute strolling along Broadway. Back at police headquarters, he was surprised to discover that the 'woman' was none other than Edward Hyde, Viscount Cornbury, late of Oxford and the Guards, former Tory MP, current Governor of New York and New Jersey, and the first – and, as far as we know, to this day the only – drag queen governor of a major American city.

Apparently his Lordship liked nothing better than to go strolling on a balmy summer evening, done up in his wife's best frock. He is reported to have stated that he would like to spend a month of every year dressed as a woman.

His penchant for cross-dressing may have been exaggerated by his enemies, but it was by no means the only odd thing about Lord Cornbury. He also harboured something of an ear fetish, and would invite guests at official receptions to fondle his wife's ears in order to establish just how 'shell-like' they were.

Regardless of his fondness for frocks (harmless enough, after all) his Lordship was certainly one of the worst British governors ever. He was staunchly corrupt – his assent could always be gained in return for a small remittance – and he was suspected of embezzling government funds, most particularly £1,500 that had been intended to improve the defences of New York harbour. American statesman George Bancroft wasn't mincing his words when he declared that Lord Cornbury demonstrated the main characteristics of the English aristocracy, to wit 'arrogance, joined to intellectual imbecility'.

Neither was he an angel at home, and Mrs Hyde's life was far from easy. Not only did her husband appropriate her best dresses, he also provided her with no money, compelling her in turn to 'borrow' clothing from other ladies. His Lordship, meanwhile, was running up ever larger debts.

Eventually the establishment had had enough of Lord Cornbury. In 1708, he was removed from office by Queen Anne and thrown into debtors' prison in London, where he languished until the death of his father, at which point he inherited his title of Earl of Clarendon and a sizeable fortune. He passed his time thereafter in the House of Lords.

Lord Clarendon died in 1723, in debt as usual, and was buried in Westminster Abbey.

A portrait, said to be of him, clad in a gorgeous blue dress and gazing alluringly at the viewer, can be seen hanging on a wall of the New York Historical Society.

94

Prince Philip:
Royal Foot in Royal Mouth

H.R.H the Prince Philip is renowned for placing his royal foot firmly in his royal mouth. Some admire him for saying what he thinks. Others cringe with embarrassment. Here are a few of his most clangerous utterances:

To a Scottish driving instructor: 'How do you keep the natives off the booze long enough for them to actually pass their test?'

To a British student in Hungary: 'You've not been here long: you haven't got a pot belly.'

To a bare-breasted Maasai lady presenting him with a gift: 'Er... you are a woman, aren't you?'

When visiting a factory in Edinburgh in 1999, on noticing a fuse box with wires unsafely sticking out: 'It looks like it had been put up by an Indian!'

During a visit to the Wesh Assembly, he was with a group from the British Deaf Association who were standing close to a band. He pointed at the musicians and said: 'Deaf? If you are near there, no wonder you are deaf.'

To British students while on a visit to China in 1986: 'If you stay here much longer you'll all be slitty-eyed.'

At the height of the recession of the early 1980s: 'Everybody was saying. "We must have more leisure." Now they are complaining they are unemployed.'

To the matron of a hospital in the Caribbean in 1996: 'You have mosquitoes. I have the Press.'

To a 1986 World Wildlife Fund meeting: 'If it has four legs and is not a chair, has wings and is not an aeroplane, or swims and is not a submarine, the Cantonese will eat it.'

To a British student in Papua New Guinea: 'You managed not to get eaten then?'

To an indigenous Australian businessman: 'Do you still throw spears at each other?'

To an inhabitant of the Cayman Islands in 1994: 'Aren't most of you descended from pirates?'

To a 13-year-old aspiring astronaut wishing to fly the NOVA rocket: 'Well, you'll never fly in it, you're too fat to be an astronaut.'

To the Nigerian secretary-general of the Commonwealth who had dressed up in his ceremonial robes for a state dinner: 'You look as if you're ready for bed.'

In the foreword to Fleur Cowles' 1987 book If I Were an Animal: 'In the event that I am reincarnated, I would like to return as a deadly virus in order to contribute something to solve overpopulation.'

To a blind, wheelchair-bound woman who was accompanied by her guide dog, in 2002: 'Do you know they're now producing eating dogs for the anorexics?'

To a Mr. Patel at a reception for 400 Indian businessmen: 'There's a lot of your family in tonight.'

93

The British Space Programme:
Crash and Burn

In December 2007 the government announced, to general bemusement, that Britain would be re-entering the space race, collaborating with the USA to crash probes onto the surface of the moon. More than one wit commented that, given the country's history of crashing spacecraft (most recently 'Beagle 2' in 2003), the new mission would be playing to our strengths.

The race to conquer the galaxy began in earnest after the Second World War, as the world's richest nations drooled at the prospect of owning nuclear-warhead-carrying rockets that could blast their enemies to kingdom come.

Great Britain, however, had shown an interest in space long before the Cold War era. The hubristically named British Inter-planetary Society was founded in 1933, and counted amongst its members the celebrated science fiction writer Sir Arthur C. Clarke – the man who first dreamed up the geostationary telecommunications satellite.

Unfortunately, science fiction is about as far as the British Space Programme ever got.

Not only did our missiles and rockets sound more like condom brands – Black Knight, Blue Streak, Black Prince… – there was the (even) more serious issue of the liquid oxygen and kerosene propellants that were used in them. The liquid oxygen could not be loaded into rockets until just before take-off, owing to the risk of 'icing'. A full fifteen minutes were required to fuel them – by which time, of course, our major cities would be heaps of irradiated rubble. Rapid response it was not.

The original British Space programme was cancelled in the early 1970s, probably not before time.

'It's utter bilge.'

RICHARD VAN DER RIET WOOLLEY, BRITISH ASTRONOMER ROYAL, TALKING ABOUT SPACE TRAVEL, JANUARY, 1956

ONE YEAR LATER THE RUSSIANS LAUNCHED *SPUTNIK*.

FIVE YEARS LATER YURI GAGARIN ORBITED THE EARTH.

THIRTEEN YEARS LATER NEIL ARMSTRONG WAS
WALKING ON THE MOON.

92

Henry 'Bunny' Austin:
Best of British… but still a Loser

Let's face it, a sportsman with the name 'Bunny' was never going to be a winner. Even in the 1920s and 1930s, when undignified nicknames were all the rage among the nation's swinging-and-flapping youth, Henry Wilfred 'Bunny' Austin must have found it hard to summon the self-respect needed to be a true champion.

'Bunny' was born in 1906 in the London suburb of South Norwood, and soon acquired his lifelong nickname, borrowed from a comic-strip character. From a very young age he was encouraged by his father to become a tennis player. The hot-housing of young players is often criticised today, but back in 1912, at the age of just six, Bunny was already a member of Norhurst Tennis club.

He was a precocious youngster, reaching a Wimbledon semi-final in 1926 while still an undergraduate at Cambridge. Six years later he made the first of his two finals, losing to an American, Ellsworth Vines, who became the world's top-ranked tennis player before losing interest in the sport and going on to achieve similar success as a professional golfer.

Alas, it was not to be thus for Bunny. In 1932 he tried changing the way he dressed on court, in the hope that he might have more success if unburdened by the traditional cricket flannels sported by male players. Bunny's move to shorts attracted much attention and set an enduring trend. Unfortunately it had no effect whatsoever on his ability to win tennis competitions.

He played in his second Wimbledon final in 1938, but his opponent, the American Don Budge, was a vastly superior player. Bunny won a mere four games as Budge steamrollered to the championship.

The following year he was the number one seed, but crashed out early in the tournament. He never played at Wimbledon again, and to this day remains the last British man to reach the ultimate stage of the competition.

91

Graham Taylor: Do I Not Like This!

The *Sun* portrayed him as a human vegetable. When England lost 2-1 to hosts Sweden in the 1992 European Championship, the newspaper headlined the victory as 'Swedes 2 Turnips 1', famously depicting Taylor's face superimposed onto a turnip. When the team lost to Spain in a friendly, he was metamorphosed into a Spanish onion.

Despite his alleged affinity with the vegetable kingdom, Taylor had been a stunningly successful club manager. He worked miracles with Watford, taking them from the Fourth to the First Division, to the third round of the UEFA Cup and to the FA Cup final, where they lost to Everton.

His promotion to national coach, however, caused disgruntlement among pundits. Taylor had never won a major honour at club level, and his 'route-one' style of football led many to question his tactical prowess. He was also slated for substituting England's leading striker Gary Lineker in a match against Sweden – not just because Lineker's goal-scoring skills were sorely needed in the game, but also because the player was just one goal away from equalling Bobby Charlton's record of 49 goals for the national side.

His England teams were consistently unimpressive. And the worse things got, the worse Taylor's language become, as caught by a Channel 4 camera crew making a documentary about the World Cup campaign. In a disastrous qualifier against Poland, after Des

Walker screwed up a pass to John Barnes, Taylor was heard to mutter, 'Ooooh, fucking... Do I not like that! What a fucking ball. What a ball, eh, from Des to Barnesy. What a fucking... It was our possession!' 'Do I not like that!' became his catchphrase.

During the crucial World Cup qualifier against the Netherlands in October 1993, Ronald Koeman, who should have been sent off earlier in the match after a cynical foul on an England attacker, scored the opening goal for the Dutch from a free kick. As the game progressed Taylor appeared to be suffering a quiet nervous breakdown on the touchline, at one point shuffling up to the linesman and telling him, 'The referee's got me the sack. Thank him ever so much for that won't you?'

Even after this debacle, there remained a slim chance for England. If Poland beat the Netherlands and England ran up a big score against San Marino, they could still qualify for the finals, to be held in the United States.

San Marino had never won an international match, but they managed to inflict the ultimate humiliation on Taylor, when computer salesman David Gualtieri scored after a remarkable 8.3 seconds – at the time of writing still the fastest goal in World Cup history. For twenty minutes San Marino were on cloud nine, until England finally woke up, in the end winning 7-1. However, the Dutch defeated the Poles, and Taylor's team made an ignominious exit from the World Cup.

Taylor resigned shortly thereafter.

'At last England have appointed a manager who speaks English better than the players.'

BRIAN CLOUGH, ON THE APPOINTMENT OF
SVEN GORAN ERIKSSON AS ENGLAND MANAGER

Edward de Vere, 17th Earl of Oxford: Better Out Than In

According to John Aubrey, the 17th century's greatest gossip (and perhaps not a totally reliable witness), Edward de Vere, a regular at the court of Queen Elizabeth I, once bowed so deeply to Her Majesty that he loudly broke wind. He was so ashamed of his indiscretion that he disappeared, spending seven years travelling the world. When he eventually returned, the Queen welcomed him back with the words: 'My Lord, I had forgot the fart!'

ACTUALLY, THE SMELL OF RALEIGH'S TOBACCO DIDN'T SEEM QUITE SO BAD NOW...

89

Maurice Flitcroft:
(Over) Par for the Course

Those twin chimeras, fame and fortune, always held an attraction for chain-smoking Barrow-in-Furness shipyard crane operator, Maurice Flitcroft. He decided that his best chance of achieving both lay in taking part in the British Open Golf Championship.

The problem was that 46-year-old Flitcroft had never really played golf. He had hit a ball around some local playing fields, but that was about it.

Undaunted, he applied to play in the qualifying event for the 1976 Open, to be played at Royal Birkdale in Southport. He prepared by borrowing a Peter Alliss instruction manual from his local library, and also studied the writings on golf technique by 1966 PGA Championship winner, Al Geiberger. Finally, using the new set of clubs he had bought by mail order, he played a lot of golf – though on a local beach rather than a golf course.

He wrote off to the Royal and Ancient for an entry form, but was disappointed to learn that amateur entrants were required to have a handicap. No problem – Flitcroft simply declared himself to be a professional.

He was instructed to turn up for a qualifier at Formby Golf Course, where he put in a performance that amazed everyone. His total of 121 – 49 shots over par – represented the worst score in the history of the British Open, and was described by one witness as 'a blizzard of triple and quadruple bogeys ruined by a solitary par.' His drive off the first tee travelled all of four feet, and was ascribed by his playing partners to nerves. After a few more shanks into the wilderness, the officials of the R&A were summoned. But since he was there legitimately, having correctly followed the procedure, there was nothing that could be done.

The next day, Flitcroft achieved one half of his ambition – he became briefly famous, dominating coverage on the back pages of the newspapers. In one memorable quote he attributed his poor play to the fact that he had left his four-wood in his car. 'I was an expert with the four-wood,' he said. 'Deadly accurate.'

Sadly, the R&A were not amused, and the following year when he applied for entry to the qualifier for the 1977 Open, Flitcroft's application was rejected.

Undeterred, he applied again in 1978, under the guise of a fictional American pro named Gene Pacecki, and played a qualifier at South Herts Golf Club. After a few holes, he was exposed and thrown off the course. In 1983, with dyed hair and false moustache, he entered yet again, this time as a Swiss golfer named Gerald Hoppy. It took nine holes before the red-faced officials worked out what was going on. In 1990 he played the Ormskirk qualifier as James Beau Jolley, making it to the third hole before once again being unceremoniously ejected.

Banned from just about every golf course in Britain, Maurice Flitcroft continued to enjoy hitting golf balls on the beaches around Barrow-in-Furness until his death in 2007

88

Squire John 'Mad Jack' Mytton: Scandalous Regency Rake

John Mytton was born in 1796, into a long line of Shropshire squires. Expelled from Westminster School for fighting with the masters, he proceeded to Harrow, where he lasted all of three days before being kicked out. A series of private tutors fared little better, not least because of Mytton's habit of playing endless practical jokes on them. On one occasion, for example, a tutor arrived back in his room to find that a horse had taken up residence there.

Despite these misdemeanours, Mytton went on to Cambridge University, accompanied by 2,000 bottles of port. Needless to say he spent more time drinking than studying, but despite this he found university life unbearably tedious, and left without graduating.

Like all wealthy young men of his time, he then embarked on a Grand Tour. On his return, he enlisted in the 7th Hussars, mainly because he liked their elaborate uniform. After the defeat of Napoleon, he returned to his estates, and at twenty-one came into an immense fortune of half a million pounds (around 40 million in today's money). Within fifteen years he had spent the lot.

In 1819 he bought his way into Parliament as MP for Shrewsbury, but for a quixotic nature such as Mytton's, politics were just too boring – he spent a total of thirty minutes at Westminster. What he did not find remotely boring, however, were horse-racing and gambling, at both of which he enjoyed some success. He also loved fox-hunting and is reported to have relished hunting naked, no matter the weather. In spite of his nudism, he is said to have owned 150 pairs of hunting breeches, 700 pairs of handmade hunting boots, 1,000 hats and 3,000 shirts. He fed his favourites among his dogs on steak and champagne, and his best horse was allowed to wander freely through his large house, Halston Hall.

Mytton scandalized society with countless madcap escapades: participating in a twenty-round bare knuckle-fight with a miner who had interrupted the hunt; arriving at a party mounted on a bear, which bit him when he tried to make it go faster; and, tragically, killing a horse by making it drink an entire bottle of port.

He treated his wives and children as badly as his animals, and his second wife ran away after he tried to drown her in a lake. (On a previous occasion, he had locked her in a room with a pack of hungry foxhounds.)

His downfall was inevitable, given his carelessness with money, memorably demonstrated on one occasion at Doncaster races when he lost £2,000, having literally thrown it to the wind. Soon the creditors were at his door, and he was forced to flee to France – in the company of an attractive twenty-year-old woman he had met on Westminster Bridge.

In France he famously tried to cure a debilitating bout of hiccups by setting his nightshirt on fire, being saved from serious injury only by an attentive servant who beat out the flames.

'Mad Jack' Mytton returned to England and died at the age of 38 in the King's Bench Debtors' Prison in Southwark in London. His life has been aptly described as 'a series of suicide attempts'.

87

Charles Ingram:
A Major Cheat

The question was: 'A number one followed by one hundred zeros is known by what name? A: Googol; B: Megatron; C: Gigabit; D: Nanomole.' For eight full minutes Major Charles Ingram dithered. His wife, Diana, in the audience, looked on in agony as he worried away at the four possibilities. He seemed about to plump for 'Nanomole' but then, out of the blue, went for 'A – Googol'. Yes, it was his final answer...

'Charles, give me the cheque for £500,000,' said host Chris Tarrant. 'You no longer have it...' Long silence and meaningful stare by Tarrant. 'You've just won a million pounds!' Cue studio audience going bonkers and Tarrant signing a cheque for a million quid.

Cue also, a few days later, a police investigation and the subsequent cancellation of the cheque with which Ingram had left the studio. It transpired that the Major had been receiving signals, in the form of coughs, from college lecturer Tecwen Whitlock, who was in the audience. For instance, question number eleven asked, 'Gentlemen versus players was an annual match between amateurs and professionals of which sport – lawn tennis, rugby union, polo or cricket?' Ingram pondered before replying, 'I think it is cricket.' This was followed by two coughs from the audience – the pair's pre-arranged signal for 'correct'. That answer took him to £64,000. On each subsequent question he was guided in the same way.

On 7 April 2003, the Ingrams and Whitlock were found guilty of 'procuring the execution of a valuable security by deception', and given two-year suspended sentences as well as being ordered to pay costs. The major and his wife declared themselves bankrupt in 2004 and he went on to write two novels. He now repairs computers for a living.

'All a trick!'
'A Mere Mountebank!'
'Absolute swindler!'
'Doesn't know what he's about!'
'What's the good of it?'
'What useful purpose will it serve?'

MEMBERS OF BRITAIN'S ROYAL SOCIETY, 1926,
AFTER A DEMONSTRATION OF TELEVISION

86

James William Davison: the Man who Held Up the Development of Musical Taste for Generations

James William Davison was *The Times'* music critic for thirty-two years, from 1846 to 1878. Though a contemporary of many of the most innovative composers in history, Davison's musical conservatism knew no bounds. It was most clearly evident in his refusal to countenance any music written since Mendelssohn. Indeed, it can be argued that he held up the development of musical taste in Britain for generations.

For instance, Davison described Tchaikovsky's *Romeo and Juliet* as 'rubbish' and declared that Verdi's *Rigoletto* 'may flicker and flare up for a few nights… but it will go out like an ill-wicked rushlight and leave not a spark behind.' Wagner's opera *The Flying Dutchman* was 'hideous'; Liszt's music was 'hateful fungi'; Berlioz was 'more a vulgar lunatic than a healthy musician'; and Schumann's entire output could 'hardly be called music at all'. Of Schubert he wrote, 'Perhaps a more overrated man… never existed'.

The only modern composer for whom Davison had any time was the Englishman Sir William Sterndale Bennett, a musical disciple of – you guessed it – Mendelssohn. In answer to those who poured scorn on his championing of Bennett, the world's worst music critic replied, 'Let posterity award to each his real deserts.'

And that it certainly did.

85=

Lianne Morgan and Michelle Stephenson: Spice-Racked

On 4 March 1994, four hundred girls who had answered an ad in *The Stage* asking, 'Are you street smart, extrovert, ambitious and able to sing and dance?' were each given thirty seconds to show why they were good enough to become a member of a new girl group. The group, which would become the phenomenally successful Spice Girls, was being put together by Chris Herbert, who along with his father Bob owned a management company called Heart. It was the age of the boy band, but the Herberts shrewdly believed that there was a gap in the market for a girl band that boys could lust after and girls aspire to be.

The successful applicants were Victoria Adams, Lianne Morgan, Melanie Brown, Geri Halliwell, and Michelle Stephenson. Herbert rented a house in Maidenhead and began to put the girls through intense rehearsals. After a couple of months it was obvious that Lianne Morgan didn't really fit in. She was shown the door and replaced by Melanie Chisholm, later known as Mel C. Morgan formed her own band, Lee Lah, and later opened a stage school.

Michelle Stephenson was also causing problems. Although she had received the highest score of all the girls at the audition, she did not seem to have the drive or the work ethic of the other girls. She was therefore asked to leave, with Emma Bunton replacing her. Stephenson claims that she actually left because her mother had been diagnosed with breast cancer, but Victoria 'Posh Spice' Beckham had a more succinct explanation: 'She just couldn't be arsed.' Stephenson went on to have a brief song-writing and session-singing career, before retiring from the music industry.

The Spice Girls, on the other hand, went on to become world-famous multi-millionaires.

SPORTY   GINGER   POSH   SCARY   LAZY

SOME MAJOR ACTS WHO HAVE NEVER HAD A UK NO. 1

OK, the number one single is devalued these days. Indeed, for some bands it never possessed any value at all. Led Zeppelin, for example, steadfastly refused to appear on *Top of the Pops* to plug their singles (although, ironically, their song *Whole Lotta Love* was used, in a cover version by C.C.S., as the theme music for the programme for many years).

The Sex Pistols also never made it. The closest they got to the chart's summit was in June 1977, when their single *God Save the Queen* arrived at number two during the week in which the Queen and a delirious country were celebrating her silver jubilee. Rumours persist that the charts were rigged that week to keep the Pistols off the top spot so as not to cause offence to the monarch.

Lots of bands had no time for the singles chart and issued singles simply as a taster for their albums and to obtain radio play, while for others it was a crucial rite of passage. It comes as a surprise to find how many big acts have never made it to number one. Here are just a few:

	Chart Hits	Highest position
Depeche Mode	50	4
Elvis Costello	37	2
The Cure	33	5
Bananarama	34	3

Billy Fury	29	2
Genesis	29	2
The Who	28	2
Texas	27	3
Squeeze	27	2
Primal Scream	24	5
Max Bygraves	23	2
Radiohead	19	3
Dire Straits	19	2
Sex Pistols	18	2
Black Sabbath	11	4

'You'll go over like a lead zeppelin'

KEITH MOON, DRUMMER OF *THE WHO*, IN 1969, TO ROBERT
PLANT, JIMMY PAGE, JOHN BONHAM AND JOHN PAUL JONES
ON LEARNING THEY WERE FORMING A BAND.

83

Peter Buckley: On the Ropes

Peter Buckley, welterweight boxer, retired from the ring in October 2008, having lost a staggering 256 of his 300 fights.

Buckley's career had started well. Following a drawn first fight and a points defeat in his second, he enjoyed a streak of six successive victories. After this, however, his career became hit-and-miss – with a great deal more miss than hit – as the defeats piled up. Remarkably, he was only stopped ten times.

The roll call of Buckley's conquerors contains many distinguished names. He lost to luminaries such as Duke McKenzie, Naseem Hamed (Buckley was the first to take him the distance) and Colin McMillan. In the course of his career, he faced – and lost to – a amazing fifteen world champions in the ring.

To the delight of the crowd, Buckley managed to win his very last fight, gaining a points victory over Matin Mohammed in his home town, Birmingham.

'Sure there have been injuries and deaths in boxing – but none of them serious.'

ALAN MINTER, FORMER WORLD CHAMPION
MIDDLEWEIGHT BOXER

82

A Flock of Football Losers

Thankfully we don't take our football quite as seriously as the Colombians, who shot dead their defender Andrés Escobar after he scored an own goal while playing against the United States in the 1994 World Cup Finals. Some howlers do, however, deserve to be punished, if only by appearing in a book like this.

Gary Sprake

Gary Sprake of Leeds United played behind one of the toughest defences in the history of the game, but he made a few errors in his time, the most notorious of which was in a league match against Liverpool in 1967. Sprake had gathered the ball and was making ready to throw it out to defender Terry Cooper, but seeing Liverpool's speedy winger, Ian Callaghan running towards him, he interrupted his throw. In doing so, however, he dropped the ball behind him and it bounced back into the empty net. Liverpool supporters, merciless as ever, launched into a chorus of Des O'Connor's chart hit of the time, *Careless Hands*.

Tom Boyd

There was good news and bad news for Scotland at the start of the 1998 World Cup in France. The good news was that they were given the honour of playing in the first match of the tournament. The bad news was that they would be playing Brazil.

At half time Scotland weren't doing badly: they'd conceded an early goal in the fourth minute but equalised through a John Collins penalty. Then, with eighteen minutes to go, the brilliant Brazilian defender, Cafu, burst into the penalty box, collected a long ball and shot. Unusually for a Scottish keeper, Jim Leighton made a brilliant save to parry the ball, but it ricocheted cruelly off Celtic captain, Tom Boyd, and over the line. Brazil won 2-1.

Samuel Wynne

You'd have thought one own goal was enough for a single match, Oldham's Samuel Wynne went one better, putting two into his own net on 6 October 1923. Wynne also had the sad distinction of dying in the service of his team. In May 1927 he suffered a fatal collapse while playing for Bury against Sheffield United. An inquest heard that he had been suffering from pneumonia.

Chris Nicholl

When Aston Villa and Leicester City drew 2-2 in March 1976, there was only one name on the score-sheet. Chris Nicholl had scored all four goals.

Brian Gayle

Sheffield United and Leeds United are sworn enemies. Imagine, therefore, how Sheffield captain, Brian Gayle, must have felt when his own goal handed Leeds the First Division Championship in 1992.

Gary Neville & Paul Robinson

In a moment that put the 'Oh, Gee!' into o.g., Gary Neville, playing for England in the vital UEFA Euro 2008 qualifier against Croatia, passed the ball back to goalkeeper, Paul Robinson. Robinson moved to kick the ball, but missed, leaving it to trickle into the net. Robinson then examined the ground as if it might hold the meaning of life, before starting to kick it in an apparent effort to smooth down the hillock (visible only to him) that had made the ball swerve so violently off-course.

Gary Mabbutt (1987 F.A. Cup Final) and Des Walker (1991 FA Cup Final)

Hats off to Gary Mabbutt, who handed the cup to Coventry with an own goal in the 1987 final, and to Des Walker, who had been a Tottenham Hotspur fan as a lad, and who, in the 1991 final, fulfilled his boyhood dream of scoring the winner for Spurs at Wembley. Unfortunately, at the time he was playing for Nottingham Forest.

John Walker: Strike a Light!

In 1826, the pharmacist John Walker accidentally brushed a stick covered in chemicals against his hearth at home, and it burst into flames. He had inadvertently invented the match.

The first recorded sale of matches was made on 7 April 1827, and within months Walker had sold 23,000 'friction lights'. They were manufactured by elderly people who lived in alms-houses close to his shop, and sold at a cost of one shilling per hundred. Each match was dipped, by Walker himself, into a mixture of antimony sulphide, potassium chloride, gum arabic and water. He called them 'Congreves' after the rocket pioneer William Congreve.

When the famous scientist Michael Faraday visited Walker to have a look at his matches, he urged him to take out a patent, but the pharmacist retorted that he was a healer of the sick, not an inventor. Inevitably, a man named Samuel Jones patented the match instead and catchily renamed them 'Lucifers'. All over Europe fortunes were made as people first copied and then improve upon Walker's match.

John Walker looked on in disdain, and in 1830 stopped selling matches in his shop.

> 'Och, we often get asked for that, but we dinnae stock it.'
>
> OVERHEARD IN A SHOP IN MORNINGSIDE, EDINBURGH

80

Whitaker Wright:
From Rags to Riches to Rags

Whitaker Wright was born in Stafford in 1846, but when his father, a Methodist minister, died in 1870, the penniless family set out to try its luck in the New World, settling in Toronto. From there Wright moved to Philadelphia, where he met and married his wife, Anna. While she was busy bearing his three children, he began accruing a fortune – for himself if not for his investors – from silver-mining companies in Colorado and New Mexico. He became chairman of the Philadelphia Mining Exchange and a major player on the New York Stock Exchange. In ten years, he earned around £200,000 – £10 million in today's terms.

In 1889 he returned to England, where he founded companies such as the British and American Corporation and the Standard Exploration Company, whose boards he filled with establishment figures who lent them a veneer of respectability.

Meanwhile Wright lived a luxurious existence in a beautiful mansion in Park Lane, throwing lavish parties to which *le tout Londres* came. He bought that ultimate symbol of great wealth, a racing yacht, and then in 1890 spent £250,000 (the equivalent of £12 million today) acquiring Lea Park and several other estates in Surrey. The property, renamed Witley Park, comprised around fourteen hundred acres of land and incorporated the lordship of the manor. Ignoring local opposition, he spent hundreds of thousands of pounds 'improving' the estate, employing six hundred workers to create a magnificent house and landscaped grounds. He added a theatre and an opulent ballroom to the house, which he decorated with valuable paintings and expensive Italian sculptures. The great architect Sir Edwin Lutyens was commissioned to design a boathouse on the estate's vast new lake, beneath which, accessed by tunnels, was a steel and glass billiards room, from where billiard players could watch fish swim past.

All of a sudden things started to go wrong. Wright had joined a team of private financiers who put up the cash for the new Baker-loo Line from Waterloo to Baker Street, an investment that failed to provide the expected return. Furthermore, following the collapse, on 28 December 1904, of his company, the London and Globe Finance Corporation, Wright was personally accused of misappropriating funds. To make matters worse, he had made illegal attempts to shore up the share price of his company.

Wright's pariah status was sealed when it was revealed that he himself had sold the bulk of his shares, investing the proceeds in substantial property holdings in and around London. In the end, however, there was no escape and he was declared bankrupt. Many people had made huge losses and there was a clamour for him to be prosecuted. A warrant was issued for his arrest.

By this time Wright had disappeared. After hiding for a week in the icehouse at Witley Park (it's not known whether jokes were made at the time about his frozen assets), he fled, first to Paris and thence to New York, where he was at once arrested and extradited back to Britain.

His trial began in January 1904 and created a sensation. An unsympathetic jury took just forty-five minutes to return a guilty verdict on twenty-four counts of falsifying balance sheets. And Wright was given the maximum sentence: seven years in prison.

After the trial Wright awaited transfer to jail in a room with his solicitor, a friend who had put up his bail, and two court officials. As they stood, shuffling their feet, Wright requested a glass of whisky and a cigar. 'So, this is British justice!' he is reported to have said as he downed the whisky, seemingly resigned to his fate.

Suddenly the colour drained from his face, his legs gave way and he collapsed heavily to the ground. Within moments he was dead. He had swallowed a cyanide pill concealed under his tongue.

The authorities informed journalists that he had died of a fit of apoplexy, and that is how the newspapers reported it the following morning. The inquest, however, revealed the truth. Whitaker Wright had swallowed enough cyanide to kill several men. As an extra precaution, he had had a loaded revolver in his pocket. On 30 January 1904, he was buried in front of more than five hundred mourners in Witley cemetery.

In October 1952, fire broke out in the grand ballroom of Lea Park, and Whitaker Wright's entire creation was destroyed.

'That insolent little ruffian, that crapulous lout. When he quitted a sofa, he left behind him a smear.'

NORMAN CAMERON, ON FELLOW POET DYLAN THOMAS

79

Gerald Ratner:
Prawn Sandwiches and 'Crap'

On 23 April 1991, at a dinner at the Institute of Directors, a prosperous and confident 42-year-old man stood up to give a speech. He looked around the room at his peers, fellow directors all (barring one or two journalists), and proceeded, with what he believed were a few humorous words amongst friends, to commit financial suicide.

Gerald Ratner, owner of the high street jewellery chain that bore his name, described his product lines to the assembled company:

> 'We also do cut-glass sherry decanters complete with six glasses on a silver-plated tray that your butler can serve you drinks on, all for £4.95. People say, "How can you sell this for such a low price?" I say, "Because it's total crap." He added that Ratner's earrings were 'cheaper than an M&S prawn sandwich but probably wouldn't last as long.'

Within days, the company had dropped in value by £500 million. As for Ratner, he lasted another eighteen months before being sacked. The Ratner name, by then synonymous with prawn sandwiches and 'crap', was consigned to retail history shortly afterwards, when the company became the Signet Group.

78

The R101 Airship: Imperial Folie de Grandeur

On 23 August 1923, the R38, the largest airship in the world, burst into flames over the Humber Estuary, killing all but five of the forty-nine people on board. Yet far from jettisoning this ridiculously flimsy and dangerous mode of transport, the Imperial Airship Scheme rapidly developed an even bigger airship, capable of carrying up to 200 troops, or five planes.

The R101 was undoubtedly a beautiful and impressive piece of engineering: 237 metres long, she had luxurious accommodation incorporated into the envelope itself, including fifty passenger cabins, a dining room seating sixty, two windowed decks for promenading, kitchens, staff quarters and a smoking room. That's right – a smoking room, on a vessel carrying 5.5 million cubic feet of hydrogen gas. It was lined with asbestos.

From the outset the R101 had all the stability of a warm jelly. During an exhibition flight at the Hendon Air Show it almost plunged into the ground, and dived repeatedly on its journey back to base. Its gas bags leaked, causing it to lose height, a tendency exacerbated by the fact that its engines were both six tons heavier than planned and prone to maniacal vibration. Nonetheless, after a few minor adjustments it was given a certificate of airworthiness, and Britain became the proud possessor of the largest aircraft ever, dwarfing even Germany's Graf Zeppelin.

The R101's maiden passenger flight to Karachi was delayed by unfavourable winds for eight days. The airship finally took off at 6.24pm on 4 October 1930. Among the fifty-four people on board were Brigadier-General Lord Thomson, Secretary of State for Air, Sir W. Sefton Brancker, Director of Civil Aviation, and Squadron Leader W. O'Neill, Deputy Director of Civil Aviation, India, as well as a phalanx of representatives of the Royal Airship Works at Cardington.

Around 2am, flying dangerously low, she was struck by violent winds over northern France that ripped off her outer covering, exposing and bursting the first gas bag. Pitching violently back and forth, she then plummeted into a hillside not far from the town of Beauvais, just north of Paris. On striking the ground, the hydrogen caught fire and engulfed the ship, killing forty-eight people.

The Imperial Airship Scheme was finally abandoned, not before time.

'Heavier-than-air flying machines are impossible.'

LORD KELVIN, PRESIDENT, ROYAL SOCIETY, 1895

77

Arthur Thistlewood:
Cato Street Cock-Up

A rthur Thistlewood's life was a catalogue of failures and disasters. To begin with, he was illegitimate at a time when such a thing mattered (though this was hardly his fault). He trained as a land surveyor, but hated the work so much that he joined the army to escape it. But he soon resigned his commission to go travelling in the United States and France. In 1797 his first wife died in childbirth, leaving him penniless. After racking up huge gambling debts, Thistlewood married again and bought a farm, which failed. In 1811 he moved to London.

Dilettante though he was, Thistlewood's travels in revolutionary France and America had sparked in him a great and genuine passion for radical politics. In London, he became an active member of a radical faction known as the Spencean Philanthropists, named after Radical democrat Thomas Spence. At night Spenceans would chalk slogans such as 'Spence's Plan and Full Bellies' and 'The Land is the People's Farm' on the walls of the capital's buildings. The authorities began to take notice of these nineteenth-century hippies-cum-graffiti-artists, and by 1816 Arthur Thistlewood was officially considered a dangerous character.

The Spenceans aspired to wrest control of the British government. To this end they organised a mass meeting at Spa Fields in London on 2 December 1816. Their somewhat vague scheme was to foment a riot at the meeting, during which they would seize the

Bank of England and the Tower of London, and thence the country. However, the police, who had prior knowledge of their plan, dispersed the meeting before anything of the sort could happen. Along with three other members of the organisation, Thistlewood was arrested for high treason. He was later released.

Terrier-like in his enthusiasm for bother, Thistlewood rapidly managed to sniff it out again after he was set free. Before his arrest, he had purchased tickets to travel to America, a journey his brief incarceration had prevented him from making. He decided to demand reimbursement for his tickets from the Home Secretary, Lord Sidmouth. A busy man who clearly thought that Thistlewood was a crackpot, Sidmouth ignored the demand. Thistlewood responded in the manner of any right-thinking person who had just escaped imprisonment for sedition. He challenged the Home Secretary to a duel.

Naturally, they locked him up. He was sentenced to twelve months in Horsham jail.

By January 1820, Thistlewood was free again, and again active in the Spencean Philanthropists. When the death of George III threw the country and the government into even more turmoil than it had been in before, the Spenceans decided to exploit the situation. A prime opportunity arose the very next month.

George Edwards, a member of the gang, had discovered that many Cabinet members were due to dine together at the Mayfair house of one Lord Harrowby. Led by Thistlewood, the Spenceans hatched a plan to invade the house, armed with pistols and bombs. With customary vagueness, they appear to have believed that this act would encourage the country to rise up with them in a popular revolution, after which they would set up a new government in Mansion House. One of their number, James Ings, a remarkably bloodthirsty coffee-shop owner and erstwhile butcher, signed up for the job of decapitating the ministers and exhibiting their heads on Westminster Bridge. As a base for their escapade, they hired a loft in Cato Street, not far from Harrowby's house in Grosvenor Square.

What the conspirators did not know, however, was that Edwards was an *agent provocateur*, sent by the government to infiltrate their organisation and incite them to take action. Thistlewood, by this time leader of the Spenceans, had made Edwards his *aide-de-camp*, even though other members were suspicious of him and sceptical of the information he had supplied.

Ignoring the fact that a servant of Lord Harrowby had informed them that his Lordship would not actually be at home that night, Thistlewood insisted on going ahead with the raid.

Naturally it was doomed. Waiting in a pub across the street from the Cato Street loft were Richard Birnie, a Bow Street magistrate, and George Ruthven, another police spy, along with twelve doughty Bow Street Runners.

At 7.30pm, the Runners burst into the loft, and a struggle ensued between plotters and plodders. Thistlewood distinguished himself by killing a Runner, Richard Smithers, with a sword, before escaping through a back window with three other conspirators. Within days, however, all four were in custody.

Arthur Thistlewood was sentenced to death for high treason. On 1 May 1820, he and his fellow conspirators were hanged and then decapitated – the punishment for treason in those days.

76

King Edward II:
Death by Red-Hot Poker

Edward II, born in 1284 to Edward I and Eleanor of Castile, was as unpopular with his barons as he was with his people. He had very little interest in ruling his kingdom, preferring to indulge his appetites in food, drink and his court favourites – Piers Gaveston and Hugh Despenser. He was also criticized for keeping company with 'buffoons, singers, actors, carters, ditchers, oarsmen, sailors and others who practised mechanical arts.'

Edward was soundly thumped by Robert the Bruce in the decisive battle of the First War of Scottish Independence, despite commanding an army three times larger than the Scottish force. Encouraged by this sign of English weakness, the Irish and the Welsh proceeded to rebel. Edward lost his French lands to Charles IV, whereupon his wife, Queen Isabella, ran off with the disaffected noble Roger Mortimer (though it is unlikely the homosexual Edward lost much sleep over this).

When Isabella landed in Suffolk with a French army in September 1326, Edward's government collapsed and the king fled to Despenser's lands in Wales. Abandoned on all sides, he was taken prisoner on 16 November and dragged off to Kenilworth Castle. Despenser was executed in grisly fashion – dragged naked through the streets, then hanged, castrated, drawn and quartered – while Edward was forced to abdicate. His fourteen-year-old son Edward III acceded to the throne, with Isabella and Mortimer pulling the strings.

Edward II, meanwhile, was transferred to Berkeley Castle in Gloucestershire, from where he managed to escape, only to be recaptured after a few weeks. A few months later, Mortimer decided to dispose of him. A set of chronicles known as *The Brut* describes his particularly gruesome murder:

When that night the king had gone to bed and was asleep, the traitors, against their homage and their fealty, went quietly into his chamber and laid a large table on his stomach and with other men's help pressed him down. At this he woke and in fear of his life, turned himself upside down. The tyrants, false traitors, then took a horn and put it into his fundament as deep as they could, and took a pit of burning copper, and put it through the horn into his body, and oftentimes rolled therewith his bowels, and so they killed their lord and nothing was perceived.

Or as Sir Thomas More later put it: 'A plumber's iron, heated intensely hot, was introduced through a tube into his secret private parts so that it burned the inner portions beyond the intestines'. When Edward III came of age in 1330, he had Mortimer executed to avenge his father's murder.

SOME MONARCHS WHO DID NOT KEEP THE THRONE WARM FOR VERY LONG

King Osbald of Northumbria (died 799)

Osbald, crowned king of Northumbria in 796, was a nasty piece of work. For a start, he was a murderer: in 780 he had burned to death Bearn, son of former King Ælfwald. He was also much criticized for his extravagant clothing and a wild hairstyle described at the time as 'pagan'. After just 27 days, he was sent into speedy exile in Pictland.

Jane Grey (c.1536-1554), Queen of England

Jane Grey reigned for just nine days from 10-19 July 1553. The great-granddaughter of Henry VII, Jane was declared queen four days after the death of her cousin Edward VI, but was soon forced to abdicate in favour of Mary I, and was incarcerated in the Tower. Sir Thomas Wyatt's rebellion in Jane's favour the following year persuaded 'Bloody Mary' that a living Jane was dangerous to have around. She was beheaded without further ado.

Edward V (1470-1483): reigned for 11 weeks, 9th April-25th June 1483

After his father Edward IV died, Edward V was left in the care of his paternal uncle, Richard of Gloucester. Instead of caring for him, he locked the boy king up in the Tower before he had even been crowned. When Parliament petitioned Richard to become king, he didn't need to be asked a second time. Edward and his brother, Richard, Duke of York, were never seen again, but are remembered as the 'Princes in the Tower'.

Harold II (c.1022-1066): reigned for 10 months, 6 January-14 October 1066

Things started well for Harold. After being crowned at Westminster Abbey, he defeated his brother Tostig and Harald Sigurdsson, King of Norway, at the Battle of Stamford Bridge in September 1066. Just four days later, however, William of Normandy landed at Pevensey and Harold marched south to engage him. On 14 October 1066, on a hill near Hastings, Harold's army was defeated. According to legend, the last Anglo-Saxon king was killed by an arrow in the eye, though some say this legend only came about because of a botched repair job on the Bayeux Tapestry.

75=

Grantley Goulding and Maureen Gardner: Track and Failed

Grantley Goulding

To compete in the first Olympiad of the modern era, held in Athens in 1896, you had to be pretty well off. In those days there were no team tracksuits, training camps or million-pound corporate sponsorship deals. You had to find your own way there and pay for your own accommodation. As a scion of a wealthy Gloucestershire family, Grantley Thomas Smart Goulding could afford it.

Goulding was in with a chance of winning gold in the first ever Olympic 110-metres hurdles. He had established a reputation as a fast and powerful hurdler in his native Gloucestershire, winning a number of races during the 1895 season, including a victory over the visiting South African champion.

In Athens, Goulding seemed to be at the top of his game. On 7 April, he easily won his preliminary heat (effectively the semifinal), beating the French sprinter Frantz Reichel into second place.

On 10 April, the day of the final, fortune seemed to be smiling on Goulding. Two of the other finalists had withdrawn: Reichel because he was serving as an assistant to Albin Lermusiaux in the marathon, and the American Welles Hoyt because he was preparing for his favoured event – the pole vault. So Goulding only had to beat Thomas Curtis of the USA to become the first ever Olympic 110-metres hurdles gold medallist.

The race seemed set to be a close one. The finalists had won their heats in exactly the same time – 18.4 seconds – and while Goulding was technically the better hurdler, Curtis was the faster sprinter.

The starter lined them up, they got on their marks and the Old Olympic Stadium went quiet. As the starter's pistol shattered the silence, the two runners burst from their crouch. Goulding stumbled as he left the blocks, immediately giving Curtis the advantage, but his strong hurdling allowed him to gain on the American as the race progressed. In the end, though, it was Curtis who clinched it, by a margin of just five centimetres. The two men had again finished in the same time – 17.6 seconds.

Goulding didn't stop running. Without hanging around to congratulate the victor or to say good bye to his supporters and team mates, he headed straight for Athens station and took the first train out of the city – stiff upper lip quivering.

Maureen Gardner

In 1948, the British government was so worried about the cost of hosting the Olympics that the flame was turned down at night to save on gas. The nation's athletes did little to lift the national mood, with Britain's paltry medal haul of three golds coming from rowing and sailing. (*Plus ça change.*)

Few gave Gardner much chance of winning a medal in her event, the 80-metres hurdles, let alone of challenging for gold. After all, she had finished only third in her heat. The firm favourite was the Dutch phenomenon Fanny Blankers-Koen, who had taken part in the high-jump at the Munich Olympics twelve years previously, and astonished the world with her announcement that she would be participating in the London games. By the time they lined up for the start, Blankers-Koen had already won the first of her four gold medals, in the 100 metres.

Right from the starter's pistol, it was a desperately close race and Blankers-Koen and Gardner crossed the line together. As the runners waited, the band began to play *God Save the Queen* and the huge, partisan crowd began to cheer – King George VI had just entered the stadium. Even Blankers-Koen seemed convinced that Gardner had won, but when the result was announced it was the Dutch athlete who was deemed the victor. They had run the race in exactly the same time, 11.2 seconds – a new world record.

The Times described Gardner's performance as 'as good a second place as ever recorded in athletics.'

73

Sir Thomas Bouch: A Bridge Too Far

When it opened in May 1878, the railway bridge over the Tay at Dundee was the longest bridge in the world, slicing an hour off the journey time between Edinburgh and Dundee. Its designer, Thomas Bouch, received for his efforts a knighthood from Queen Victoria, as well as the somewhat less coveted 'Freedom of the Burgh of Dundee'. While still in his twenties he had invented the roll-on-roll-off train ferry, a design still in use today. He had also been involved in many important rail projects, responsible for cost-saving innovations that allowed small companies to play a part in the expansion of Britain's adolescent rail network.

So what is Bouch doing in the loser bin?

The building of the Tay Bridge was a massive project. The North British Railway Company had decided to build an uninterrupted railway line from London to Aberdeen, necessitating the construction of bridges across the Firth of Tay and the Firth of Forth to bypass the unreliable and slow train ferries that were at the time the only means of crossing the estuaries. The Tay Bridge was the first of these, with Bouch appointed to design the project.

The foundation stone was laid on 22 July 1871, but problems arose almost immediately. The surveyors had failed to notice that the bedrock in the estuary had sunk so deep in places that it could not serve as a foundation for the bridge's piers. Bouch was forced to revise his plans to reduce the load placed on the foundations. His original brick piers were replaced with cast iron columns, placed at far wider intervals, and set deep into the estuary bed. The railway company's insistence that costs be cut meant that much of the foundry-work was of poor quality.

Nevertheless, the bridge was completed in six years, only a little behind schedule. It was two miles long, with 85 spans and, like almost all of Bouch's bridges, it was constructed of lattice girders supported on slender cast iron columns, braced with wrought iron struts and ties. The train ran through a tunnel of 27-foot 'high girders', 88 feet above the water.

The first train crossed on 26 September 1877 and in May 1878 the bridge was officially opened. It received the royal seal of approval when Queen Victoria rode across in June 1879. Bouch began preparations for the bridge over the Forth.

However, on the night of 28 December 1879, a storm ravaged Scotland. In the Tay estuary, a force-ten gale blew at right angles to the new bridge. At 7.15 pm, as a passenger train was crossing, the wind proved too much for the structure. Its 'high girders' gave way, and the train plunged into the Tay. Seventy-five people were drowned in the icy waters, with only 46 bodies recovered.

The inquiry found that the bridge was 'badly designed, badly built and badly maintained', and that its downfall was due to 'inherent defects'. Bouch had not made allowances for wind pressure in his calculations for the new iron columns and longer girders – indeed, at the time it was not customary to do so – and he had used brittle cast iron for vital joints. Moreover, the structure had been of uneven thickness, the bridge had been poorly maintained and trains had been travelling over it at 40mph rather than the advised 25. The shoddy practices of the railway company were condemned, but Bouch was held personally to blame for the disaster.

Like his bridge, Thomas Bouch collapsed, and was ordered by his doctor to take a complete rest. A few months later, he caught a severe cold and died, aged 57, on 30 October 1880, his reputation in tatters.

72

Cuthbert Burnup:
A Complete Amateur

Cuthbert James 'Pinky' Burnup was an amateur sportsman *par excellence*, playing both cricket and football at the end of the nineteenth century. He played his cricket for Kent, and turned out on the wing for Cambridge University and Old Malvernians.

While playing for the MCC in 1900, Burnup entered the history books by bowling a ball that was hit for ten runs – a record score off a single ball in first-class cricket.

Perhaps unsurprisingly, Burnup was never selected to play cricket for England. In football, though, he was called up for international duty on one notable occasion, in April 1896. The England football team had gone twenty matches without defeat, a run that had begun in March 1890. The next match was against Scotland at Celtic Park, but two of the English stars – halfback Ernest 'Nudger' Needham of Sheffield United and Steve Bloomer, one of England's greatest ever strikers – had dropped out through injury. They were replaced by Harry Wood and 20-year-old Cuthbert Burnup.

Wood's inclusion was unpopular, but Burnup's selection was universally condemned as evidence of a dual bias: both towards players from the south, and towards amateurs. The outcry proved justified. England's unbeaten run ended in a galling 2-1 victory for the Scots, and Burnup's performance was so bad that it at last galvanised the Football Association into ending its longstanding reliance on amateurs.

71

Arup, Foster and Partners and Sir Anthony Caro: the Wobbly Bridge

On 10 June 2000, two months late and £2.2 million over budget (not bad for a piece of modern British civil engineering), a new footbridge known as the Millennium Bridge opened. Built by Monberg Thorsen and Sir Robert McAlpine to designs by Arup Foster and Partners and Sir Anthony Caro, it crossed the Thames from St Paul's to the Tate Modern art gallery.

Two days later, on 12 June 2000, it closed for modifications. The problem? It wobbled.

In the intervening days the gleeful public had flocked in their thousands to experience the infamous wobble for themselves. Writing in *The Times*, Libby Purves commented that the sight of the queues made her proud to be British.

The bridge finally reopened in February 2002, *sans* wobble.

70

The 2006/7 England Cricket Team:
The 'Whitewash' Ashes Series

It had been a mere fifteen months since that memorable, sun-splashed September evening at the Oval, when England won the Ashes for the first time since 1987.

Yet here they were in Sydney in January 2007, losing the fifth test on the fourth day by 10 wickets and suffering a whitewash defeat (5-0) against the Australians for the first time since the tour of 1920-21.

England had chucked away the last five wickets for a paltry 45 runs in just 15 overs. The Aussies, requiring only 46 runs to win the test and complete the embarrassment of the whitewash, managed to get the job done before lunch.

HOWZAT! SOME RECORDS FROM THE WHITEWASH SERIES

In the first innings of the First Test, Australia took a first-innings lead of 445 runs, after making 602 for 9 (declared) and dismissing England for 157. Ricky Ponting, the Australian captain decided against the follow-on, electing to bat, instead. Their resulting 445-run lead was the largest ever in Test history where the follow-on has not been enforced.

England's first innings score in the Second Test, 551 for 6, was the highest score ever achieved by a team batting first and electing to declare – only to lose the match.

Australian batsman Adam Gilchrist's second-innings century in the Third Test, off only 57 balls, was the fastest century in an Ashes Test, and the second-fastest in any Test (the West Indies' Viv Richards did it off only 56 balls, also against England, in 1986).

During his innings, Adam Gilchrist scored 24 runs off Monty Panesar in a single over – an Ashes record.

The fifteen months England held the Ashes (the Australians took the series when they won the third Test) was the shortest period any of the two teams has ever held the urn.

SOME OTHER LAMENTABLE CRICKETING RECORDS

The lowest scores in First-Class English county cricket

12 runs	Oxford University (v MCC)	1877
	Northamptonshire (v Gloucestershire)	1907
13 runs	Nottinghamshire (v Yorkshire)	1901
14 runs	Surrey (v Essex)	1983
15 runs	MCC (v Surrey)	1839
	Northamptonshire (v Yorkshire)	1908
	Hampshire (v Warwickshire)	1922
	(Hampshire still won!)	
20 runs	Sussex (v Yorkshire)	1922
	Derbyshire (v Yorkshire)	1939

The two worst overs by an English bowler in a test match

Bowler: Ian Botham
Season: 1980-81
Runs scored: 25 (4-6-2-6-6-L)
Batsman: Andy Roberts (West Indies)

Bowler: Andy Caddick
Season: 2001-02
Runs scored: 25 (6-6-6-NB/L-4-1-0)
Batsman: Nathan Astle/Chris Cairns (New Zealand)

Hit for six... six of them!

While playing for Nottingahamshire, the West Indian legend, Gary Sobers, hit six sixes in one over bowled by Malcolm Nash of Glamorgan at Swansea on 31 August 1968. In 1977, Nash was hit for 34 runs in one over by Frank Hayes of Lancashire.

Losing Without Taking a Wicket

In 1956 Leicestershire lost to Lancashire without taking a single wicket in the entire match. Leicestershire won the toss and chose to bat first, scoring 108. Lancashire declared at 166 without loss. In the 2nd innings, Leicestershire scored 122. Lancashire scored the 64 required to win, again without loss.

Useless With the Bat

In 1930, Seymour Clark, a local club cricketer in Weston who was a train driver with the Great Western Railway, was called into the Somerset side for five matches when regular wicket-keeper Wally Luckes was taken ill. Clark did not waste the opportunity: he created a record for the most innings without scoring a single run – 9 in five matches. *Wisden* recorded in his 1996 obituary that Essex and England bowler, Peter Smith, attempted to give him a run in a match that Essex were winning convincingly. He bowled so gently that the ball bounced twice before getting to Clark. He was still bowled out by it.

 In 1990, Mark Robinson of Northamptonshire recorded the longest sequence of innings without scoring – 12. His scores that season were: were 1, 0, 1, 0, 0, 0, 0, 0, 0, 0, 0, 0, 0, 0, 0 and 1.

69

Unity Mitford:
Hitler's Other Woman

Once described by Adolf Hitler as a 'perfect specimen of Aryan womanhood', the Honourable Unity Valkyrie Mitford was – so the story goes – conceived in the Ontario mining town of Swastika, where her family owned the Swastika Mine.

Unity was the fourth of the six Mitford sisters, famed variously for their beauty, literary success and extreme politics. The Mitford parents, the 2nd Baron and Baroness Redesdale, were supporters of Sir Oswald Mosley's British Union of Fascists, and their daughter Diana married Mosley in 1936. Unity went one better. She turned her back on the indolent life of a debutante and travelled to Germany, where she became a relentless stalker. The object of her obsession? Adolf Hitler himself. She would turn up in the restaurants he ate in, and lurk near him at political rallies.

Eventually he took notice of the leggy blonde in the low-cut blouse. She became a favoured member of his inner circle. Hitler was entranced by her Teutonic middle name and her grandfather's friendship with his idol, Richard Wagner, and Unity spent summers at his house in the country. Hitler's girlfriend Eva Braun resented their friendship, writing of Mitford, 'She is known as the Valkyrie and looks the part, including her legs. I the mistress of the greatest man in Germany and the whole world, I sit here waiting while the sun mocks me through the window panes.' Braun reportedly tried to regain her place in Hitler's affections by attempting suicide.

Unity passionately shared the Nazis' hatred of the Jews. The British Secret Service reported that she was 'more Nazi than the Nazis' and she once gave the Nazi salute to the British Consul General, who immediately took steps to have her passport impounded. She was blind to the horrors perpetrated by the Hitler regime. 'Poor sweet Führer,' she wrote, 'he's having such a dreadful time.' Not as bad a time as the eighty-five close friends and supporters whose deaths he had just ordered in the Night of the Long Knives.

As war approached, Unity found herself in a precarious position. Should she remain in Germany and stay true to her beliefs, or should she return to her homeland and betray her principles? She did neither. Instead, on 3 September 1939, the day that Prime Minister Neville Chamberlain declared war on Germany, she sent a letter to Hitler, took the pearl-handled pistol that he had given her, and went to the English Garden in Munich. She put the pistol to her head and pulled the trigger.

The bullet failed to kill her, but it did cause brain damage. Amidst calls for her to be imprisoned as a traitor, Unity was sent back to England, where she lived out the rest of her days in the care of her mother at the family home in Oxfordshire. The *Daily Mirror* asked why 'the Mitford girl, who has been openly consorting with the King's enemies, should go scot free.' Rumours abounded that the bullet wound was a ruse to get Unity back to England without suffering the consequences of her involvement with the Nazis, although these were vociferously rebutted by her sisters.

Incontinent and with a mental age of twelve, Unity spent the rest of her life an invalid. Aged 33, she died from meningitis, arising from an infection resulting from her brain injury.

In 2007 an article appeared in the *New Statesman* detailing rumours that when Unity returned home she was pregnant with the Führer's son. The child was allegedly given up for adoption.

Needless to say, the story has never been proved.

'It was the most wonderful and beautiful day of my life. I am so happy that I wouldn't mind a bit, dying. I'd suppose I am the luckiest girl in the world. For me he is the greatest man of all time.'

UNITY MITFORD, AFTER MEETING HITLER FOR THE
FIRST TIME, 1934

68

Derek Redmond:
Pop Goes the Hamstring

Derek Redmond was good. As a member of the British men's 4 x 400 metres relay team, he had won several gold medals, and was among the favourites for the 400 metres individual gold in Barcelona. Granted, he had been dogged by injury throughout his career – in Seoul in 1988, he had been forced to withdraw just ten minutes before the race due to an Achilles injury, and by the time he arrived in Barcelona he had endured eight operations – but he was in the best form of his life. And he was absolutely focused on winning a medal.

Things started well. In the first round, he recorded the fastest time of all the competitors, and he followed that up by winning his quarter-final heat. On the day of the semi, 65,000 excited spectators packed the stands of the Estadi Olímpic de Montjuïc. Among them was Redmond's father Jim, watching nervously from the top row.

As the athletes hit the back straight, Redmond was amongst the front-runners. On the form he had been displaying, he looked like an excellent bet for the final. But suddenly he began to pull up. In the commentary box, David Coleman screamed, '... and Derek Redmond has broken down... the jinx has struck again!' Redmond hopped forward a couple of steps, clutching the back of his thigh, but it was no good. He had distinctly heard something pop in his leg. It was the sound of his hamstring snapping.

He crouched on the track, distraught, hands covering his face as the other runners crested the bend and crossed the finishing line on the far side. But as the stretcher bearers ran towards him, he struggled to his feet and, with the crowd going wild, began to hobble round the track in a courageous attempt to finish the race. At the final bend, however, a scuffle broke out behind him, as a man wearing a 'Just do it' baseball cap and a tee-shirt bearing the legend 'Have you hugged your foot today?' ran onto the track. It was Jim Redmond, shouting, 'That's my son out there. I'm going to help him.' Unceremoniously shoving the officials aside, he caught up with Derek, put an arm around his shoulders and helped him along the track. More officials approached. Jim told them in no uncertain terms to go away.

Together, father and son crossed the line, providing one of the great moments in British Olympic history.

Jim Redmond later said simply: 'We started his career together and I think we should finish it together.'

General Sir John Cope:
Hanoverian Humiliation

The Battle of Prestonpans was the first conflict of any significance in the second Jacobite rebellion, when troops led by Charles Edward Stewart ('Bonny Prince Charlie') rose up against the English King George II. The battle, fought on 21 September 1745, ended in humiliating defeat for General Sir John Cope, commander-in-chief of the King's army in Scotland.

On 2 July 1745 Cope had received an unconfirmed report that the Jacobite pretender was about to arrive in Scotland with the objective of raising support for a bid for the crown. He pressed the Secretary of State for Scotland, the Marquess of Tweeddale, to recall all officers from leave and bring the army's horses in from pasture, but Tweeddale, anxious to avoid panic, demurred. It was only when the Bonny Prince had actually landed on the Hebridean island of Eriskay that the government finally authorized Cope to prepare his troops.

Leaving half his men at Stirling, Cope marched the rest north to Fort Augustus to secure the stategically vital chain of forts that stretched from Inverness to Fort William. The presence of a government force would, he reasoned, deter wavering Highlanders from joining the rebels. At the same time he hoped to reinforce his own small army with members of clans loyal to the government. Once this had been achieved, he would confront the enemy.

The ovens at Leith, Stirling and Perth were set to work round the clock to produce 21 days' supply of bread for the marching army. Once baked, however, the bread had to be transported north. Therein lay the problem. A paucity of baggage horses meant large quantities had to be left behind. Of the loaves that did set out, thousands were stolen *en route*, and the rest arrived too late to salvage the plummeting morale of Cope's troops. Large numbers of the Black Watch deserted.

To make matters worse, support for the king's forces from the Highland clans was weaker than anticipated, with prevaricating clan chiefs using every possible excuse to delay their men from joining up. Others did not bother to prevaricate, telling Cope to his face to get lost. The general, under direct orders from Tweeddale to proceed whatever the circumstances, pressed on.

On 26 August, he received the disappointing news that the rebels had taken the Corrieyairack Pass that led over the mountains to Fort Augustus. Knowing that it would be impossible to retake the pass, he marched his men to Inverness, again hoping to raise troops from the local clans. He prayed that the rebels would pursue him, so that he could face them in a set-piece battle that he could be confident of winning.

As before, the chieftains were reluctant to provide him with troops. All he got were 200 men from the Munro clan, and he had those for just two weeks. Meanwhile, instead of chasing Cope as he had hoped, the rebel army turned to march on Edinburgh.

Cope reckoned that the quickest way to the capital would be to travel by sea to the port of Leith from Aberdeen. Seven days later, on 15 September, the army set sail for Leith on boats commandeered for the purpose. Again his luck was out. The wind blew steadily in the wrong direction and he was unable to enter the Firth of Forth. He was forced to disembark his army at Dunbar, twenty miles east of Edinburgh, which had fallen to the Jacobites that very day. He chose to make his stand at the small town of Prestonpans.

Cope's defensive position appeared to be a good one, with two stone walls on the right, a marsh on the left, the sea behind and a deep ditch in front. He also far outgunned the Scots with his six one-and-a-half-pound guns and six mortars. The enemy, in contrast, was forced to bolster their meagre quantities of guns and swords with axes and pitchforks.

On the eve of the battle, the Jacobite rebels learned of a hidden path through the bog and, under cover of darkness, silently manoeuvred their way along it. At dawn the Highlanders attacked, engaging the English in hand-to-hand combat, a type of fighting at which they excelled. The government dragoons and foot soldiers fled, abandoning their artillery, while the Scots put to death every Englishman they could find. Prince Charlie galloped amongst them pleading with them to stop the killing – after all, he regarded Scots and English alike as his rightful subjects.

General Cope fled to Berwick-upon-Tweed, where he had to suffer the ignominy of reporting his own defeat. He would never again command an army in the field, and to this day the Scots sing a song dedicated to his disastrous performance at Prestonpans:

> *Hey, Johnnie Cope, are Ye Waking Yet?*
> *Are your drums a-beating yet?*
> *If you were waking, I would wait*
> *To gang to the coals in the morning.*

Of course, in the end the Bonnie Prince was an even bigger loser, but Cope surely deserves honourable mention.

66

Dorothy Squires:
Marital Bondage

Tinseltown is a cruel place. When British singing sensation Dorothy Squires visited Hollywood in the company of her young actor boyfriend Roger Moore in 1954, she found herself the subject of a barrage of malicious jibes. 'Don't forget to invite Roger Moore and his mother' was one of the not-so-hilarious jokes doing the rounds of that age-obsessed community. (Moore was – gasp – twelve years her junior.)

By the time he met Dorothy, Roger had already been married, to a fellow student at RADA – the beautiful Doorn Van Steyn, who combined thespian skills with a talent for ice-skating. She too had been older than him (by six years) and their relationship was combustible. Stitching together a living as a knitwear model and film extra, Moore shared a single room in Streatham with Doorn, her parents, her brother and her two sisters. Not surprisingly the marriage began to fall apart. On one occasion she lay in wait for him at the stage door of the Lyric Theatre, biting him when he emerged.

He may have considered himself lucky, therefore, when he made the acquaintance of Dorothy Squires one evening in 1952, at a party at her house. Sensationally, the aspiring actor and the recording star were soon an item.

At the start of their relationship, Dorothy was a huge star. Her big break had come when she hooked up, romantically as well as professionally, with accordion-playing bandleader and songwriter,

Billy Reid. Abandoning his wife and kids, Billy moved in with Dorothy and wrote numerous hits for her, making her Britain's most popular female singer. Despite the success, their relationship was tempestuous. Squires later claimed that when she was on tour Reid would climb a ladder up to her hotel-room window to make sure she was sleeping alone. By the time she met Moore, she had had enough. Reid was out of her life.

The bandleader was heartbroken when he learned of her impending marriage to Moore, even writing another two hint-laden hits for her – *I Still Believe (We Were Meant For Each Other)* and the ultra-creepy *I'm Walking Behind You (On Your Wedding Day)*.

Moore and Squires were married in the United States, and his career – benefiting not a little from his wife's fame – began to take off. There were rows, however, not helped by his philandering, and in the end he fell for 28-year-old Luisa Mattioli, his co-star in a low-budget Franco-Italian toga saga, *The Rape of the Sabine Women*. By this time Dorothy was 46, eighteen years older than her paramour's new love. She first heard about Mattioli from their doctor, and some letters she intercepted from Italy confirmed the worst.

Dorothy went to pieces, and in a bizarre move sued Moore very publicly for 'restitution of conjugal rights'. When that failed, she refused to grant him a divorce for seven years. She later threatened to publish an autobiography that would include not only transcripts of Moore's love letters to her, but also those from Luisa to Moore that Dorothy had got her hands on. Worse still, there would be graphic accounts of her sex life with Moore. Needless to say, and sadly for lovers of the seamier side of celebrity, an injunction prevented the book's publication.

Dorothy became very familiar with the courts. Having launched 33 legal actions following her bankruptcy in 1986, she was eventually declared a vexatious litigant by a judge and barred from the courts. A couple of years later she was evicted from her 17-room mansion in the beautiful Berkshire village of Bray.

The last ten years of Dorothy Squires' life were spent in penury, but she did have the grim pleasure of seeing Moore do to Luisa what he had done to her, when he left her for the Swedish socialite, Christina 'Kiki' Thorstrup.

In April 1998, when 83-year-old Dorothy was in hospital dying of cancer, Moore called her niece, Emily, and asked her to 'take hold of her hand, give it a little squeeze, and tell her Rog is thinking of her.'

65=

Deborah Kerr and Richard Burton: I'd Like to Thank the Academy... for Nothing

Deborah Kerr, Scottish-born star of stage, television and film, was nominated for a Best Actress Oscar a remarkable six times in eleven years, but she never got the chance to make that tear-drenched speech. Hollywood covered its embarrassment by giving her a consolation award in 1994.

Welsh icon and serial Elizabeth-Taylor-wedder Richard Burton was also nominated six times for Best Actor, but never won. Neither did he pick up the Best Supporting Actor Oscar when he was nominated for *My Cousin Rachel*, making him a seven-time loser. This record is surpassed only by Irish actor, Peter O'Toole, who has been nominated for eight Oscars – though, like Deborah Kerr, he received an honorary Oscar. Burton did not.

Deborah Kerr's Six Nominations

1949 *Edward, My Son*
1953 *From Here To Eternity*
1956 *The King and I*
1957 *Heaven Knows, Mr. Allison*
1958 *Separate Tables*
1960 *The Sundowners*

Richard Burton's Six Nominations

1953 *The Robe*
1964 *Becket*
1965 *The Spy Who Came In From the Cold*
1966 *Who's Afraid of Virginia Woolf*
1969 *Anne of the Thousand Days*
1977 *Equus*

63

William Henry Ireland: Shakespeare Hoaxer

In the eighteenth century Shakespeare first achieved the cult-like status he still enjoys today. His plays were staged constantly and collectors searched fanatically for relics of the bard. Yet, to their intense frustration, there was almost nothing in the actual handwriting of the great playwright – no surviving letters to his friends, patrons, publishers or associates. Of the thirty-seven plays that he had authored, not a single copy was in his own hand.

Samuel Ireland was a travelogue publisher and collector of antiquities, as well as of Shakespeare plays and memorabilia. His son, William Henry, grew up in a world of books, and was particularly captivated by the sensational story of Thomas Chatterton, who had hoodwinked the literary establishment with his forged, supposedly medieval poems, before committing suicide in 1770 at the age of just seventeen.

In 1794 William Henry brought home a document from the law office where he worked. He explained to his delighted father that it was a mortgage document signed by Shakespeare himself, claiming that it had turned up amongst the papers of a client who wished to remain anonymous. Over the following weeks he brought a series of Shakesperean documents home, including several notebooks and a love letter to Anne Hathaway, as well as the twin holy grails of Shakespeariana – the original manuscripts of *King Lear* and *Hamlet*.

William Henry, of course, had forged the lot, but his father Samuel was overjoyed. Experts were also taken in, and the documents were authenticated by assorted scholars. In 1796 Samuel Ireland published a lavishly illustrated set of facsimiles.

At this point the scam became still more ambitious. William Henry 'discovered' an entirely unknown Shakespeare play – *Vortigern and Rowena* – the rights for which were acquired by the Irish playwright Richard Brinsley Sheridan for £300 (equivalent to around £17,000 in today's money). It was staged at London's Drury Lane Theatre on 2 April 1796. The performance was an utter disaster.

If the actor-owner of the theatre, John Philip Kemble, had his doubts about the play's authenticity, the cast knew perfectly well it was a fake, and expressed their derision by hamming it up outrageously throughout the performance. When the fateful line, 'And when this solemn mockery is ended', was delivered by Kemble, there was uproar in the theatre, as the audience erupted into laughter and rapturous applause.

A few weeks later William Henry confessed all, but to his dying day his father believed the documents were genuine.

His reputation ruined, William Henry Ireland lived out the remainder of his life in poverty.

'Who is this Pope that I hear so much about? I cannot discover what is his merit. Why will not my subjects write in prose? I hear a great deal too of Shakespeare, but I cannot read him. He is such a bombast fellow.'

KING GEORGE II ON ALEXANDER POPE,
WILLIAM SHAKESPEARE AND POETRY IN GENERAL

62

John Otway:
The Man who made Failure a Career

Singer-songwriter John Otway's embrace of loserdom is truly heroic. In 1977 the tsunami of Punk was obliterating everything in its path. The Sex Pistols were growling anarchy from the speakers of the nation's radiograms, while The Clash injected 'attitude' into the British youth. Otway did not fit this mould. He sounded like Eddie Grundy of *The Archers*, and looked like the rock dinosaurs Punk was set on blasting to extinction. Nevertheless, he reached 27 in the charts with the song *Really Free*, a love-song (of sorts) with the charming chorus: 'Cor baby, that's really free'.

Then... nothing. His first album bombed, even though Pete Townsend of The Who twiddled the controls. A string of follow-up singles failed miserably. Undaunted, Otway persisted, eventually building a loyal fanbase with his self-deprecating humour and his athletic, often downright dangerous performances. He was rewarded in 2002, when a concerted campaign put his song *Beware Of The Flowers Cause I'm Sure They're Going To Get You, Yeah* at number seven in a BBC poll to find the greatest lyrics of all time.

Asked the same year what he wanted for his 50th birthday, Otway said he would like to have another hit record, and thus remove for all time the stigma of 'one-hit wonder' from his name. His fans obliged, propelling his song *Bunsen Burner* to number nine in the charts. At last John Otway, prince of losers – and proud of it – was able to release a Greatest Hits album.

'There's no point in success if you don't let it go to your head. That's what it's for."

JOHN OTWAY

61

Stanley Green:
Protein Wisdom

For twenty-five years, from 1968 until 1993, Stanley Owen Green fought a losing battle against passion. Or rather, against protein. The billboard that he sported six days a week on Oxford Street bore the unequivocal message: 'LESS LUST, BY LESS PROTEIN: MEAT FISH BIRD; EGG CHEESE; PEAS BEANS LENTILS'. Appended to the placard, as something of an afterthought, was 'AND SITTING'. His general approach was elegantly summed up by two words beneath those: 'PROTEIN-WISDOM'.

Born in 1915, Green spent the Second World War in the navy, where he was profoundly shocked by the lewd talk of his fellow sailors. By an inscrutable process of logic, he came to believe that their obsession with sex was the result of eating too much protein. In an effort to suppress his own sexual desires, he lived on a diet of porridge, home-made bread, steamed vegetables and pulses.

He worked variously for the Fine Art Society, Selfridges, the civil service and Ealing Borough Council, before finding his true vocation as a full-time human billboard in 1968. Every day he cycled the twelve miles from his flat in Northolt to central London, where he would march up and down Oxford Street, bearing his placard. His strenuous efforts were not always welcomed by passers-by, and his importuning of young women led on occasion to his arrest. He took to wearing green overalls to protect himself from the spit that was often directed at him.

Green's message was elaborated in a 14-page pamphlet – *Eight Passion Proteins*, of which he is said to have sold 87,000 over the years (to the intense irritation of his neighbours, these were all noisily printed in his flat on his day off). Other literary works remained unpublished, such as his novel, *Behind the Veil: More than Just a Tale*, and the expanded, 392-page version of *Eight Passion Proteins*, which Oxford University Press unaccountably declined to publish in 1971. Meanwhile, letters flew from his passionless pen to Prince Charles, five Prime Ministers, the Archbishop of Canterbury and Pope Paul VI, amongst others.

Stanley Green died in 1993, leaving behind a Britain as passionate and lustful as ever it had been.

60

Sir Freddie Laker:
The People's Champion

All those lucky people shuttling to and from their *gite* in the Dordogne on Ryanair should say a tiny prayer of thanks to Freddie Laker every time they book a ridiculously cheap flight. For it was Laker, a former war-surplus aircraft dealer, who in the 1970s first opened our eyes to the dizzying possibilities of cheap air travel with his airline, Laker Airways.

His 'Skytrain' fares across the Atlantic were a third of the price charged by the major airlines which had so long had a stranglehold on long-haul travel. Before Skytrain, the International Air Transport Association had permitted the major airlines to maintain an inefficient monopoly. They offered more or less identical services at inflated prices.

Sadly, Laker Airways went spectacularly bankrupt in February 1982 with debts of more than a quarter of a billion pounds. Some of the blame can be put down to over-ambitious expansion, but there is little doubt that the major airlines conspired against Laker in the same way they later did against Sir Richard Branson's Virgin Atlantic and Sir Stelios Haji-Ioannou's Easyjet, matching his prices at their own loss in order to put him out of business.

The largest anti-trust case in aviation history was launched against ten major airlines in America. It was settled out of court.

59

Anonymous British Ambassador
to Mexico

This may be too good to be true, but why let the truth get in the way of a good story?

One recent festive season, the British ambassador to Mexico (let's maintain his anonymity) was asked by a Mexican television station what he would like for Christmas. Naturally this caused great consternation, as the ambassador wrestled with the ethical conundrum thrown up by receiving a gift from a media outlet. After lengthy consultation with senior members of his staff, he settled on a modest, uncontroversial request.

On Christmas day His Excellency was seated in front of the television when he heard the newsreader announce, 'And finally, we asked the ambassadors to our country what they would like for Christmas. The French ambassador said he wished for world peace. The Canadian ambassador requested a cure for cancer. The British? A small box of crystallised fruits.'

58

King Charles I:
Failed to Keep his Head

Did a king ever do so much to get up the noses of his subjects? Charles I seems to have set out to give himself royal grief. For a start, at a time when Catholics were about as welcome in England as a skunk at a garden party, he married one – Henrietta Maria, fifteen year-old daughter of Henri IV of France. Then, to placate his wife and her family, he refused to help the Protestant Huguenots against the army of the new French King, Louis XIII.

Parliament took revenge by refusing to levy taxes to pay Charles enough to keep himself in stiff collars and beard wax, handing over £150,000 instead of the million quid he wanted. He sent the Parliamentarians away to spend more time with their families.

The royal coffers remained as empty as a politician's promise, however, forcing him to invite MPs back from their estates. But all they did on their return was complain about him, so he told them to get lost again.

Next, he came up with a wizard wheeze – he would revive the ancient custom of Ship Money, tax levied from coastal towns, usually when England faced foreign invasion. 'Er, what foreign invasion would that be?' was the complaint of sheriffs up and down the coast. When Charles went back to the seaside towns for more the following year, there was big trouble.

He was forced to recall Parliament for the third time in his five years as king, and when they resolutely refused to hand over any more cash, he tried to dissolve the sitting yet again. The MPs grabbed the Speaker and locked the doors. Charles responded by imprisoning several of them. There would be no more Parliaments for eleven years, during which Charles irritated the Scots by meddling in their religious affairs, leading them to invade England. With no money, he was unable to raise a decent army and had to pay them off from his limited funds and promise to keep his nose out of their business in future.

In 1640, Parliament was again summoned. This time it lasted twenty years, inevitably becoming known as the Long Parliament. Determined to bring the king into line, it executed one of his chief advisers without trial. Charles tried to have five of his opponents arrested, which was the final straw for the Paliamentarians. They formed their own army whereupon Charles fled London for Oxford to raise *his* own army. It was game on.

Three years later, at Naseby, after the Royalist forces were on the wrong side of a crushing defeat, Charles fled to Scotland. The Scots had long memories, however, and handed the king over to Parliament in January 1647. He was imprisoned at Hampton Court, but escaped in November of that year, raising another army and persuading the Scots to fight on his side. As ever, the Scots were happy to do anything that annoyed the English, but Oliver Cromwell finally defeated them in August 1648 and Charles found himself again in Parliamentarian custody.

On 30 January 1649, after a trial at which he refused to defend himself, claiming superciliously that he was God's representative on earth, King Charles I mounted the scaffold outside Whitehall Palace, where his head was chopped off. Only later did they notice that he was wearing two shirts, apparently so that no one would see him shivering from the January cold and mistake it for fear.

57

Frederick, Prince of Wales:
He was alive and is Dead

Frederick, Prince of Wales, was born in Germany into the House of Hanover. When he was just seven, his parents upped sticks and headed for Britain, forgetting to take him along.

When he turned up in 1728, a fully-grown man, they refused to have anything to do with him, referring to him as a 'foundling'. And when his father George II was told that 'Poor Fred' had been taken ill one night, his reply was: 'I hope it's nothing trivial.'

The public liked Frederick, however, and a famous epitaph describes their feelings about his dysfunctional family.

> *Here lies poor Fred*
> *Who was alive and is dead*
> *Had it been his father*
> *I had much rather*
> *Had it been his sister*
> *Nobody would have missed her*
> *Had it been his brother*
> *Still better than another*
> *Had it been the whole generation*
> *So much better for the nation*
> *But since it is Fred*
> *Who was alive and is dead*
> *There is no more to be said!*

'I come from a family of losers, and I've rejected my family as something I don't want to be like.'

STING, TALKING HIMSELF OUT OF A FAMILY CHRISTMAS

56

George Mallory:
Did He or Didn't He?

The debate continues as to whether George Mallory and his young climbing partner, Andrew Irvine, reached the top of Mount Everest in June 1924.

In May 1999, Mallory's body was finally found. Face down in the snow, it was 26,760 feet up the mountain's north face – 2,269 feet from the top. But the piece of evidence that could decide the case has yet to be unearthed. Mallory's Kodak camera, which would certainly contain pictures taken on the summit, had he reached it, is still somewhere on the mountain.

Whatever the truth, the question remains – can reaching the top of a peak but failing to get back down again be described as a successful climb. Sir Edmund Hillary, who most definitely did make it both there and back again, put it this way: 'I am rather inclined to think personally that maybe it is quite important, the getting down, and the complete climb of a mountain is reaching the summit and getting safely to the bottom again.'

His romantic death apart, Mallory led an extraordinary life. The son of a Cheshire clergyman in 1886, he showed early climbing prowess on the roof of his father's church. At thirteen he won a mathematics scholarship to Winchester College, where his teacher Graham Irving, a daring climber, introduced Mallory to mountaineering on an expedition to the Alps. He had discovered his passion in life.

After reading history at Cambridge, Mallory lived in France for a while, returning in 1910 to take up a teaching post at Charterhouse, one of England's leading public schools. He married in 1914, just as the First World War broke out, and enlisted as a second lieutenant in the Royal Garrison Artillery. On 16 June 1915, he was wounded in the leg during an attack on German trenches at Ypres and was sent home. At the end of the war, he returned to Charterhouse, but found himself restless and unhappy. In 1921, he resigned, and joined the first Everest expedition.

He had devoted much of his spare time to climbing. In 1911 he reached the top of Mont Blanc, and made the third ever ascent of the difficult Frontier Ridge of Mont Maudit. Two years later he climbed the Pillar Rock in the Lake District unaided, creating a route now recognised as 'Mallory's Route' – for a long time considered the hardest climb in Britain. Even Geoffrey Winthrop Young, one of the top Alpine climbers of the day, was in awe of Mallory's almost superhuman prowess as a climber:

> 'His movement in climbing was entirely his own. It contradicted all theory. He would set his foot high against any angle of smooth surface, fold his shoulder to his knee, and flow upward and upright again on an impetuous curve. Whatever may have happened unseen the while between him and the cliff... the look, and indeed the result, were always the same – a continuous undulating movement so rapid and so powerful that one felt the rock must yield, or disintegrate.'

The 1921 Everest expedition was a reconnaissance mission whose aim was to explore routes up to the mountain's North Col. Mallory was instrumental in drawing up the first accurate maps of the area around the mountain, laying the foundations for the first serious attempt on the summit of Everest the following year.

General Granville Bruce led the expedition, and Mallory almost made it to the top, ascending the North-East Ridge to a record altitude of 26,985 feet without oxygen. A few days later another party, using oxygen, broke that record, reaching a height of 27,300 feet. Indomitable as ever, Mallory resolved to make a new attempt, even though the monsoon was beginning to make conditions very difficult. As they waded through waist-high snow on the North Col, the party was struck by an avalanche that killed seven of the Sherpas acting as their guides. The expedition was abandoned, and on his return home Mallory was harshly criticised for risking an attempt on the summit in deteriorating conditions.

He took a job with the Cambridge University Extramural Studies Department, but left to join General Bruce on the fatal 1924 Everest expedition. On 8 June, after a trek of two months from Darjeeling to the camp on the North Col, with supplies running low, members of the expedition ailing from oxygen sickness and snow blindness, and bad weather closing in, Mallory and fellow climber Andrew Irvine embarked on their last ascent to the summit.

Did they reach the top? There is no firm evidence that they got any further than the area on the mountain known as the First Step, but Noel Odell, a geologist on their expedition, reported seeing them through a break in the clouds, high on the mountain on the Second Step. In his estimation they were three hours from the summit:

> 'My eyes became fixed on one tiny black spot silhouetted on a small snow-crest beneath a rock-step in the ridge; the black spot moved. Another black spot became apparent and moved up the snow to join the other on the crest. The first then approached the great rock-step and shortly emerged at the top; the second did likewise. Then the whole fascinating vision vanished, enveloped in cloud once more.'

It was the last time Mallory and Irvine were seen alive.

Another tantalising piece of evidence was furnished by one of Mallory's daughters, who said that he had taken a photograph of his wife with him to leave at the top of the mountain. His body and garments were well preserved by the permafrost, yet no photograph was found among them. Had he deposited it on the summit?

Britain, of course, did what it does best, rapidly alchemising the lead of failure into the gold of eternal glory. Mallory's memorial service at St Paul's Cathedral was attended by the great and the good: King George V and most of the Royal Family were there, as were Prime Minister Ramsay Macdonald and the entire cabinet.

Thus ended the earthly existence of George Mallory, perhaps the quintessential Great British Loser.

55

Maurice Wilson:
At Least He Felt Successful

A rather different character who also lost his life in the attempt to conquer Mount Everest was the soldier, mystic, mountaineer and aviator, Maurice Wilson. This decorated hero of the First World War launched an extraordinary bid to climb the mountain in 1934, despite having no mountaineering experience whatever.

After the war Wilson had led a peripatetic lifestyle, dogged by physical and mental illness, until an encounter with a mystery medical man in Mayfair effected a miracle cure. His treatment included 35 days of intensive prayer and fasting, after which Wilson became a fervent advocate of such methods. So fervent, indeed, that he became convinced that these disciplines alone would enable him to launch a successful assault on the world's highest mountain. His plan was to fly a plane into the upper slopes of Everest and simply to walk to the summit from the crash site. His complete lack of flying experience was merely one of many trifling objections that, to Wilson, were unworthy of consideration.

In the end he was persuaded to embark on a course of flying lessons, taking an inordinate amount of time to gain his pilot's licence. He then bought a three-year-old Gypsy Moth, naming it *Ever Wrest,* but promptly crashed it in a field near Bradford. The crash came to the attention of the Air Ministry, which immediately forbade him from flying to India as he had planned.

Wilson took no notice, and set off for the Himalayas on 21 May.

All along his route the British government made efforts to stop him, withdrawing permissions to fly over territories and withholding fuel where he landed. Nevertheless, he made it to India, only to be informed by the authorities that he would not be permitted to fly over Nepal. They even impounded his plane to make certain he did not even try.

Wilson wintered in Darjeeling, recruiting three Sherpas to help him the following spring. On 21 March, disguised as monks, he and the Sherpas left Darjeeling. On 14 April they arrived at the Rongbuk Monastery – a well-known stopping-off point for Everest climbers – and Wilson set off alone to climb the mountain. Nine days later, defeated by the arduous climb up the Rongbuk Glacier, he arrived back at the monastery.

On 12 May he set off again, this time taking two of the Sherpas with him. A few days later, they reached Camp Three, beneath the North Col.

After a couple of unsuccessful attempts to climb a forty-foot ice wall that was difficult even for experienced mountaineers, let alone a complete novice, the Sherpas pleaded with him to give up and return to Darjeeling. The stubborn Wilson refused. On 29 May, with the parting words, 'This will be my last effort and I feel successful,' he launched his final assault on the mountain. He never returned.

The following year Maurice Wilson's body was found at the foot of the North Col.

54

Marianne Faithfull:
Pop Siren but Loser in Love

The tempestuous relationship between Mick Jagger and Marianne Faithfull provided tabloid fodder in abundance in the late 1960s. Suicide attempts, betrayals, drug busts, confectionery... it had them all.

The pair met at a Rolling Stones party in 1964. The beautiful 17-year-old was launching herself as a singer, and Jagger, Keith Richards and producer Andrew Loog Oldham wrote the winsome ballad *As Tears Go By* for her. It was the first of many hit singles. In 1965 Faithfull married the artist John Dunbar, owner of the Indica Gallery – where John Lennon would later meet Yoko Ono – and gave birth to their son Nicholas. Thanks to Dunbar's heroin addiction, however, the marriage was brief, and Faithfull sought refuge at the house of Rolling Stone Brian Jones and his girlfriend Anita Pallenberg. She soon began her notorious relationship with Jagger.

Faithfull's background is exotic compared to that of Dartford Grammar School boy Jagger. She is the daughter of Major Glynn Faithfull – an army officer, spy and university professor – and Baroness Eva Erisso, who in her younger days had been a ballerina and had worked with Bertolt Brecht. On her mother's side she is descended from Baron Leopold von Sacher-Masoch, author of the erotic novella *Venus In Furs*, from whose surname the word 'masochism' was coined. Her paternal grandfather invented a sexual device known as the Frigidity Machine.

It is little surprise, therefore, that Faithfull stood out amongst the other girls on the scene. As Loog Oldham put it: 'At a time when most chicks were shaking ass and coming on strong, here was this pale, blonde, retiring, chaste teenager looking like the Mona Lisa, except with a great body.' Her awkward, bookish beauty inspired Bob Dylan to write a long poem for her while she was visiting him in the Savoy Hotel, though he tore it up when he could neither talk her out of her impending marriage nor into his bed. She became Jagger's muse, and songs such as the beautiful 'Wild Horses' were written with her in mind. By December 1966, they were a couple.

Soon drugs began to play a major part in Faithfull's life and in February 1967 she and Jagger were caught up in the legendary drugs raid on Keith Richards' Sussex house, Redlands. From this emerged the infamous Mars Bar story (denied by all parties, of course). Myth or not, it only added to the aura of decadence surrounding the couple. In 1968, addicted to cocaine, Faithfull suffered a miscarriage.

Meanwhile the hits had dried up, and she took up acting, while her life and relationship continued to fall apart. She began abusing barbiturates and alcohol, and in 1969 almost died in Australia. She and Jagger were due to start filming *Ned Kelly* when she overdosed on Tuinals. The couple remained together for another year, but Faithfull was in freefall. Strung out on heroin, she once fell asleep in her soup at a dinner at the house of the Earl of Warwick. Amid the tumult of drugs and infidelities, the end of their relationship finally came in May 1970, when Jagger moved to France to escape the UK's draconian tax regime. His first child was born six months later, to American singer and actress Marsha Hunt.

When she read in a newspaper about Jagger's marriage to Bianca Rose Perez Moreno de Macias in May 1971, Faithfull got so drunk she was arrested in an Indian restaurant in Chelsea. She told a reporter, 'Even if I died or [Mick] died, I still won't get away from him. We can't get away from each other by dying.'

'I'd rather be dead than singing Satisfaction
when I'm 45'

MICK JAGGER, 1970

53

The Creators of BBC One's *Eldorado*, Britain's Worst Ever Soap Opera

Ham acting, wooden scripts, no storylines – these were some of the nicer things the critics had to say about the 1990s BBC soap, *Eldorado*. Filmed in a purpose-built £2-million village constructed in the south of Spain, it would last just a year before it was put out of its misery by the incoming Controller of BBC One, Alan Yentob.

During its run viewers had been flummoxed by bits of unsubtitled dialogue in languages from Spanish to Danish. Not to mention a cast of actors who themselves seemed utterly baffled by what was going on around them.

Among those who emerged from the wreckage with their previously spotless reputations somewhat tarnished were Julie Smith and Tony Holland, who had had created *Eastenders*, and the executive producer, Verity Lambert, who had been involved in the early stages of *Doctor Who*.

'Television won't last. It's a flash in the pan.'

MARY SOMERVILLE, PIONEER OF RADIO
EDUCTATIONAL BROADCASTS, 1948

52

The Scotland Football Team:
Losing All Over the World

Saturday 15 June 1996. The old Wembley Stadium was filling up for the first round of Euro '96. Scotland were to face the Auld Enemy – the England who had defeated them so many times throughout the centuries, while the Scots had only the odd upset to their credit, a few rare Bannockburn moments. More often it was Flodden and Culloden – backs to the wall, lambs to the slaughter, and so on. The Scots are masters of loss, doyens of disaster. Failure is built into the Scottish psyche, programmed into their synapses. Yet always there was some kind of saving grace: they were outnumbered, they lost gallantly, they nearly did it…

At Wembley, the Status Quo classic *Rocking All Over the World* rang out from the end where the Scottish legions stood. But one word of the song had been altered, turning it into a unique celebration of defeat – *Losing All Over the World*.

As usual the lyrics proved apt. Scotland lost two-nil. Gary McAllister did miss a penalty though, and I'm sure I saw the English keeper move before the kick was taken…

Another glorious defeat.

ENGLISH FOOTBALL
LOSING RECORDS

Biggest Losers:

Halifax Town lost 13-0 to Stockport County in the Third Division North on 6 January 1934.

Newport County lost 13-0 to Newcastle United in the Second Division on 5 October 1946.

Most losses in a season

Doncaster Rovers, playing in the old Third Division, lost 34 matches in season 1997-98. They managed to win 4 and draw 8.

Lowest number of paying spectators

There were more players on the pitch than paying spectators when Stockport County took on Leicester City on 7 May 1921. Just thirteen people turned up to watch the match which, to make matters worse, was played at Manchester United's vast Old Trafford stadium, Stockport's ground being temporarily unavailable.

51

William Huskisson: the World's First Railway Accident Victim

William Huskisson achieved a great deal in politics and finance, but it is the unfortunate manner of his death that makes him a regular topic in pub quizzes.

After nine years in France, where he witnessed first-hand the start of the French Revolution, Huskisson returned to England in 1792. His knowledge of politics and finance caught the attention of Prime Minister William Pitt the Younger, and he held a string of important posts in the Tory government. He helped to establish free trade, and was instrumental in toning down the inflammatory Corn Laws.

Yet if Huskisson had hoped to gain eternal fame for these endeavours, his efforts were to no avail. On 15 September 1830, he was attending the opening of the Liverpool and Manchester Railway, the world's first inter-city passenger service. At Parkside, near Newton-le-Willows, he got out of his train, the *Northumbrian*, to pay his respects to the Prime Minister, the Duke of Wellington, who was in a nearby carriage. As he picked his way up the track, he failed to notice another train – the *Rocket* – approaching from the other direction. Notoriously clumsy, Huskisson lost his balance and fell onto the rails. His leg was crushed, and after hours of agony he died at nine that evening.

So William Huskisson went down in history as the first person ever to be run over and killed by a train.

'Rail travel at high speed is not possible,
because passengers, unable to breathe,
would die of asphyxia.'
DR DIONYSYS LARDER (1793-1859),
PROFESSOR OF NATURAL PHILOSOPHY AND ASTRONOMY,
UNIVERSITY COLLEGE LONDON

50

British Airways: A Tail of Two Logos

In 1997 British Airways launched a brand-new tailfin design, created by a trendy London agency. Their previous logo, deemed arrogant, imperialist and worst of all uncool, was replaced with ultra-hip images by international artists.

Unfortunately the removal of the Union Jack from BA tailfins ruffled the feathers of many, not least the air traffic controllers, who claimed they were unable to identify the fleet in its cool new livery. None other than the hand-bag wielding ex-PM Margaret Thatcher came charging back into battle. 'We fly the British flag, not these awful things,' she told the embarrassed airline officials who had invited her to view models displaying the new design. She then delved into the famous handbag and extracted a hand-kerchief, which she draped over the offending tailfin.

As ever, Richard Branson, boss of rival Virgin Atlantic, was quick to exploit the situation. He had the Union flag added to all his planes and cheekily lifted British Airways' former slogan, 'Fly the flag'.

In May 2001, Chief Executive Rod Eddington announced that the entire BA fleet would have Union flag livery put back on its tailfins.

OTHER BRITISH BRAND DISASTERS

Consignia

By 2000, the name 'Post Office' had served the public well for 300 years, but it was not good enough for the blithering idiots who ran the organisation. Deciding that the Post Office was about more than just post and that its name should reflect that fact, they came up with 'Consignia' because… well, because it had 'consign' in it. They also pointed to its suggestive royal connotations (it sounds a bit like the word 'insignia'). The public thought it sounded more like aftershave or deodorant, and when business turned bad, the name was blamed. In May 2002, Consignia was consigned to history.

Coco Pops

There was national uproar in 1998 when breakfast cereal behemoth Kellogs made the rash decision to re-name its cocoa-flavoured version of Rice Krispies in the United Kingdom. The name they chose was Choco Krispies, bringing it into line with the one used in much of the rest of the world. Astonishingly, a million people took part in a telephone poll in which 92% of respondents demanded the return of the old name. Coco Pops were back on the shelves within a year.

Lymeswold Cheese

Advertising agencies often turn out cheesy ads, but in 1981 one agency went a step further and churned out an actual cheese. That year, a restructuring of the Milk Marketing Board's activities had led to the creation of the 'Dairy Crest' brand, whose purpose was to use surplus milk production in the manufacture of other products. The guys in the shiny suits were summoned, in the form of the ad agency Butler, Dennis & Garland, and were given a brief. They decided, perhaps as they gazed at the cheese board at the end of an expenses-paid lunch, that what was missing from the British dairy offering was a soft blue cheese. No problem. They invented a village – Lymeswold – and created Lymeswold cheese, a soft, mild blue cheese with an edible white rind. On the back of heavy promotion, demand initially outstripped supply, but the new cheese on the block soon gained a reputation for poor quality, and in 1992 Dairy Crest ceased production. The news was greeted by the restaurant critic of the Daily Telegraph, and no doubt many others, with 'unfettered joy'.

Persil Power

In the early 1990s, multinational Unilever was striving to gain an edge over its competitors in the fiercely competitive detergent market. To this end they created a new catalyst that improved the cleaning performance of their powder, even at lower temperatures. Not wanting to interfere with their main product, and mindful of disasters such as 'New Coke', they packaged the catalyst as an entirely new product which could be added to normal Persil in varying amounts, depending how tough the stain was. They called it Persil Power.

A huge marketing campaign launched Persil Power, but the product soon ran into trouble. The first problem was that normal Persil dealt with most stains perfectly well. More critical was the fact that after Persil Power had been used a few times, clothes began to lose their colour and fall apart. It emerged that these effects had not been apparent on the new clothes used by Unilever in tests, but that older clothes were actually destroyed by it. Persil Power was recalled and the brand was washed down the plughole.

Dasani

Early advertisements in Coca-Cola's 2004 £7-million launch campaign for the new branded water, Dasani, labeled it as 'bottled spunk' and featured the tagline 'can't live without spunk', seemingly oblivious to the British slang meaning for that particular word. In fact, the water turned out to be nothing more than Sidcup tap water, purchased at 0.03p a half litre, treated, then sold under a fancy name for 95p per half litre. Coke claimed that it underwent a sophisticated purification process based on NASA spacecraft technology, but it emerged that the process was the same as the one used in many domestic water purification units. In March 2004 Dasani was found to contain the suspected carcinogen bromate, at which point it rapidly disappeared from the supermarket shelves.

'If Richard Branson had worn a pair of steel-rimmed glasses, a double-breasted suit and shaved off his beard, I would have taken him seriously. As it was I couldn't...'

LORD KING, CHAIRMAN OF BRITISH AIRWAYS

49

Bonny Prince Charlie: Derby and No Further

Bonnie Prince Charlie and his army of Highlanders had reached Derby – these days just a short National Express coach ride from London – when they suddenly lost their nerve. Unbeknownst to them, utter panic reigned in the capital as its terrified citizens awaited rape and pillage by a rabid host of kilt-wearing maniacs. The streets emptied, there was a run on the banks as people stuffed their cash under their mattresses and into their corsets, and King George II's packed suitcases stood by the door in readiness for flight back to his native Hanover.

The prince was all for pressing on from Derby, but the clan chieftains, led by Lord George Murray, brother of the Duke of Athol and an experienced soldier, voted to turn round and return to Scotland.

*

Prince Charles Edward Louis John Casimir Sylvester Severino Maria Stuart was born into privileged exile in Rome in 1720, the grandson of King James II and VII of England and Scotland, who had reigned for four years before being kicked out by the Glorious Revolution of 1689. Ever since, the Jacobites had been struggling to restore the Stuarts to the throne.

In 1743 Charles was named Prince Regent by his father, and a fresh Jacobite campaign was launched. Eighteen months later he had raised sufficient funds to equip a mere three ships for battle.

After one failed attempt at invasion, when his tiny fleet was sent packing by the British near Torbay, the Bonnie Prince decided that his only chance of success was to raise a rebellion in Scotland first. He landed on the Hebridean island of Eriskay, from where he sent messages to the clan chiefs asking for their support. Most told him to get lost, but he remained resolute, believing the Highlanders would come out in droves when they got wind of his arrival.

He raised the standard at Glenfinnan on 19 August 1745 and waited for the clans to arrive. For three hours nothing happened, then slowly they began to show up, kilts swaying, bagpipes skirling.

When the government in London placed a price on his head, Charles responded by offering the same for the capture of the man he called the 'Elector of Hanover' – King George II. He led his army to Perth, and on 16 September marched into Edinburgh.

Charles remained in Edinburgh for six weeks, basking in the adoration of the people of that fair city – especially the women. He then marched into England, taking Carlisle on 17 November. As he continued onward to Manchester, however, he was disappointed by the paltry numbers of Englishmen rallying to his standard. Still, on 5 December they arrived in Derby. London was now just a few days' march away.

At this point things started to go wrong. Intelligence was received that the King's son, the ruthless and obese William, Duke of Cumberland, was leading a force of 10,000 men in their direction. The Jacobites turned and began to march back to Scotland.

On 16 April, 1746, after a lacklustre siege of Stirling Castle, the Jacobite army faced the government troops at Culloden, a few miles east of Inverness. The Highlanders were routed, and Charles famously fled in drag, with the help of his faithful Highlanders and Flora MacDonald. By September 1746 he was back in France, and the Stuart cause was forever lost.

Bonnie Prince Charlie died in Rome on 31 January 1788, by which time he was styling himself 'Count of Albany'.

48

Sir Arthur Conan Doyle: Fairies at the Bottom of the Garden

Sir Arthur Conan Doyle was sickeningly talented. As well as the great Sherlock Holmes and Dr. Watson, he created marvellous characters such as Professor Challenger and Brigadier Gerard. He also wrote a number of historical novels, and some of the best short stories in the English language. Not only that, he was also a fine sportsman, and once took the wicket of the great W.G. Grace in a cricket match. He played football, rugby for Portsmouth, and was responsible for introducing cross-country skiing to the Swiss, who for some reason hadn't already come up with the idea themselves.

He also believed in fairies.

Modern spiritualism had emerged in western New York State in the mid nineteenth century, in response to a widespread craving for tangible proof of the afterlife. This area was home to rabidly religious immigrant Swedenborgians, Mesmerists and other zealots. To these enthusiasts, such 'proof' duly arrived in the form of the Fox sisters, who claimed to communicate with the ghost of a peddler who had been murdered in their house. He communicated, they said, with taps, knocks, automatic writing and – when his spirit chose to occupy one of their bodies – by voice.

The Fox sisters became famous, and soon others began to imitate them, charging people for communicating with loved ones on the 'other side'. At séances, tables would move and tilt, a cold breeze would blow on the faces of participants, flowers would appear out of thin air, ghostly music would play, and the medium would appear to become the channel for ghostly voices.

Even when one of the Fox sisters confessed that their communication with the dead peddler was fraudulent, and that they had created the mysterious noises by cracking their toe-joints, spiritualists – Conan Doyle amongst them – refused to believe that the escapade on which their entire movement was founded was a hoax. Conan Doyle went so far as to write: 'Nothing that she could say in that regard would in the least change my opinion, nor would it that of any one else who had become profoundly convinced that there is an occult influence connecting us with an invisible world.'

How did such an intelligent man fall for such nonsense? In his defence, he had suffered a series of losses. His first wife, Louisa, had died in 1906, and between 1916 and 1919 he lost his son Kingsley, his brother Innes, two brothers-in-law and two nephews. Spiritualism gave him reassurance – he needed to believe in an existence beyond the grave.

The matter caused a very public falling out between Conan Doyle and his friend Harry Houdini, the great American escape artist and magician. Houdini loathed spiritualism, and merrily seized every opportunity to expose fraudulent Spiritualist mediums. Despite this, Conan Doyle was convinced that Houdini himself – who openly admitted that his feats were mere tricks – possessed magical powers, and wrote about it in his book *The Edge of Unknowing*.

But it was the Cottingley Fairies that showed the full extent to which Conan Doyle believed in this mumbo-jumbo.

In 1917, two Yorkshire girls – sixteen-year-old Elsie Wright and her cousin Frances Griffiths, aged ten – claimed to have taken photographs of fairies in their garden. Their pictures show tiny winged people floating in the air, playing flutes and dancing on leaves. To modern eyes the fakery is pretty obvious – the wings are not blurred with movement even when the fairy in the photograph is suspended in mid air, for instance. The girls maintained the veracity of the pictures until 1982, when they at last admitted in an interview that they had faked them using cardboard cutouts. Frances said in the interview: 'I never even thought of it as being a fraud. It was just Elsie and I having a bit of fun and I can't understand to this day why they were taken in. They wanted to be taken in.'

Conan Doyle was among those who swallowed it hook, line and sinker, going so far as to write two pamphlets and a book – *The Coming of the Fairies* – claiming they were genuine. The great novelist G.K. Chesterton summed it up thus: 'It has long seemed to me that Sir Arthur's mentality is much more that of Watson than it is of Holmes.'

HOLMES MADE A MENTAL
NOTE TO ASK WATSON WHERE
HE'D PURCHASED THIS LAST
BATCH OF TOBACCO

47

Edward VII:
Brainless Bertie

Edward VII had a lot of time on his hands. Known to the Royal Family as 'Bertie', he was heir to the throne for 59 years and 74 days, longer than anyone in British history until Prince Charles came along. (At the time of writing, Charles has been heir apparent for 59 years and 195 days.)

Bertie whiled away the years by having a good time. When he was finally crowned king in 1901, his mistresses were allotted a special area in Westminster Abbey, which was referred to as 'The King's Loose Box'. He also did his dynastic duty, of course, fathering five new members of the Royal Family from his marriage to the charming and beautiful Queen Alexandra.

At heart, though, he was a playboy.

In Paris, where he spent a great deal of time, he was once introduced to the actress Giula Barucci, known as 'the greatest whore in the world'. She curtsied and then let all her clothes fall to the floor, leaving her completely naked in front of the prince. He also had relationships with Sarah Bernhardt, the great Spanish courtesan 'La Belle Otero', the actress Lillie Langtry, Lady Randolph Churchill (Winston's mother), socialite Alice Keppel, Daisy Greville, Countess of Warwick and the wealthy humanitarian Agnes Keyser. He even once dallied with a cockney prostitute, Rosa Lewis, in the back of a hackney carriage.

The last time he saw his father, Prince Albert had reprimanded him because fellow officers had hidden an actress by the name of Nellie Clifton in his tent during army manoeuvres in Ireland. Albert died two weeks later, and Queen Victoria blamed Bertie. 'I never can, or shall, look at him without a shudder,' she wrote.

BERTIE ARRIVES IN PARIS

46=

Kevin Maxwell and William Stern: Filthy Lucre

Kevin Maxwell

When media tycoon Robert Maxwell went for a permanent dip off the side of his yacht, the *Lady Ghislaine*, his son Kevin must have felt that he was the one drowning. Within a short while he had become Britain's biggest ever personal bankrupt, indebted to the tune of no less than £406.5 million. Maxwell signed on the dole, then somehow proceeded to become a director of twenty-four companies, eight of which soon underwent insolvency proceedings. He also set up telecoms business Telemonde, which defaulted on payments worth £54 million, although Maxwell narrowly avoided being made bankrupt for a second time in 2004.

William Stern

Until Kevin Maxwell outdid him in the bankruptcy stakes, former refugee William Stern had held the unenviable title of Britain's biggest bankrupt. In 1974 his company, the Freshwater Group, sank with debts of around £143 million. Five years later Stern joined it when he went personally bankrupt to the tune of £118 million. Either history does repeat itself or Stern was so arrogant that he chose not to learn from his mistakes, because he did it all over again when his second property empire went into liquidation with debts of more than £14 million.

The judge, banning him from being a director for twelve years, described him as 'fundamentally irresponsible'.

A BEVY OF BRITISH BANKRUPTS

Michael Barrymore (1977 and 2004)

Following the discovery of the body of 31-year-old Stuart Lubbock in his swimming pool in March 2001, Barrymore's entertainment career imploded. He was declared bankrupt after receiving a bill from the Inland Revenue for £1.4 million of unpaid tax.

Lionel Bart (1972)

The *Oliver!* composer went bust when he tried to shore up two musical flops with his own money. He took to the bottle and suffered from depression for the next twenty years. He died in 1999.

George Best (1982)

The brilliantly talented Northern Irish footballer spent much of his fortune on booze and Miss Worlds. The rest, as he liked to say, he squandered...

Jim Davidson (2006)

Four marriages, five children and a declining career led to the foul-mouthed comic being declared bankrupt, with £700,000 owed in taxes. As if that wasn't bad enough, in 2003 he was voted number 20 in a Channel 4 poll of the 100 Worst Britons, and in 2007 was asked to leave Gordon Ramsay's celebrity cooking show *Hell's Kitchen* on Channel 4 after making homophobic comments about fellow B-list celeb Brian Dowling.

Daniel Defoe (1692)

The writer of *Robinson Crusoe* went under with a wife and seven children to support. He was continually falling into debt, having bought a country estate, a ship and a bunch of expensive cats, as well as embarking on a series of doomed mercantile ventures.

Chris Eubank (2005)

The lisping former World Super-Middleweight Champion hit the canvas owing £1.3 million in taxes.

Edward II (14th century)

War against France put him £30 in debt, which is more than £3,000,000 in today's money.

Adam Faith (2001)

The actor/singer/financial journalist, who had an early hit entitled *What Do You Want If You Don't Want Money*, was declared bankrupt owing a reported £32 million after the failure of the Money Channel, in which he had an interest.

Keith Floyd (1996)

Married and divorced four times, the late TV chef Floyd was declared bankrupt while running the Floyd's Inn pub in Devon, reportedly after he had personally guaranteed a booze order for £36,000 – a hell of a round of drinks, even by his bibulous standards.

George Frideric Handel (1737)

When Handel's music slipped out of fashion, he filed for bankruptcy and became depressed. As if that was not bad enough, he then had a stroke and his fingers became crippled. Nonetheless, a couple of years later, he made a stunning comeback by composing the eternally popular oratorio *Messiah*.

William Roache (1999)

When the *Sun* alleged in 1992 that Bill Roache, who has played the character Ken Barlow in *Coronation Street* for almost fifty years, was 'boring', Roache sued for libel. Unfortunately, when the newspaper offered to settle out of court with a payment of £50,000, Roache's lawyer Peter Carter-Ruck, advised him to reject the offer. They went to court. He won damages of £50,000, but because he had rejected the settlement, he was liable for his own costs, a not-inconsiderable sum. Roache sued Carter-Ruck for giving him bad advice, but lost – an unsurprising outcome when suing the country's leading libel lawyer. Facing debts of £300,000, Roache declared himself bankrupt in 1999.

Oscar Wilde (1895)

When the playwright dropped his libel case against the Ninth Marquess of Queensberry who had accused him of sodomy, the Marquess, father of Wilde's paramour Lord Alfred Douglas, obtained a judgement against Wilde for the full repayment of the £600 he had spent on his defence. Wilde was declared bankrupt.

44

The Light Brigade:
A Magnificent Charge, but not War

Take a badly worded order, add a soupçon of idiocy, a pinch of personal antagonism and a good measure of plain pig-headed stubbornness – historically not in short supply in the British army – and you have a recipe for glorious disaster. A great many men displayed a great deal of courage on 25 October 1854, but the entire escapade was more *Carry On* farce than military manoeuvre.

The infamous charge took place during the Battle of Balaclava in the Crimean War, while the Russians were making the first of two attempts to break the siege at Sebastopol. The Earl of Lucan, in command of the cavalry, received an order from the commander of the army, Lord Raglan, which read:

> *Lord Raglan wishes the cavalry to advance rapidly to the front, follow the enemy, and try to prevent the enemy carrying away the guns. Horse artillery may accompany. French cavalry is on your left. Immediate.*

Captain Louis Nolan who delivered the order, stressed that the cavalry should attack at once, so Lucan ordered Lord Cardigan and his cavalry forward into the valley. Lucan himself intended to follow with the Heavy Brigade.

Raglan's aim was to prevent the Russians from removing the naval guns from the Causeway Heights on the *left* side of the valley. However, when Lucan asked for clarification as to which guns were meant, Captain Nolan made a vague sweeping gesture that seemed to indicate the Russian guns at the far end of the valley, a mile away.

Hence the 673-strong Light Brigade set off towards the Russians' 5,000 men and 50 artillery pieces, lined up at the end and on either side of the valley. Suddenly Nolan galloped across in front of Cardigan. Had realised that the Light Brigade was charging at the wrong target? We will never know, as he was hit by an artillery shell, and became the Charge's first victim. The Light Brigade continued on its disastrous course.

The fire from three sides began to decimate them, but they managed to push the Russian forces back before heavy losses forced them to retreat. Meanwhile Lucan had held back the Heavy Brigade, claiming later that he saw no reason why another force should be wiped out by the Russian artillery. Some suspected, however, that his long-term animosity towards his brother-in-law Cardigan was the true reason.

Cardigan, meanwhile, had led the charge from the front, reached the Russian guns and returned up the valley, oblivious to what had happened to his men. Later, he said that he was preoccupied by his rage at Captain Nolan, who had, he believed, tried to take over at the front of the charge when he had darted forward. He left the battlefield, boarded his yacht in Balaclava Harbour and had a good dinner, washed down with champagne.

In the aftermath, all parties blamed each other for what had turned out to be an almighty, tragic cock-up. One hundred and fifty-six men died, 122 were wounded and only 195 of the original 673 had horses at the end of it. The Russians were so astonished by the manoeuvre, they presumed the British were drunk. The French Marshal Pierre Bosquet commented: 'C'est magnifique, mais ce n'est pas la guerre.' ('It's magnificent, but it isn't war.') What is rarely quoted, however, is the last part of what he said: 'C'est de la folie!' ('It's madness!')

43

Squadron Leader Archibald Stuart Maclaren, Flying Officer William Noble Plenderleith and Sergeant W.H. Andrews: Intrepid 'Never-Say-Die' British Aviators

In March 1924 Squadron Leader Archibald Stuart Maclaren, Flying Officer William Noble Plenderleith and flight engineer Sergeant W.H. Andrews set out from Calshot Spit, an RAF seaplane base near Southampton, intending to record the first ever round-the-world flight in their Vickers Vulture amphibious biplane. A fourth member of the team, Lt. Colonel L.E. Broome, remained in England to supervise the logistics of the trip.

The plan was to set off over France and Italy, then cross the Mediterranean to Cairo. From there they would wing their way to India, Burma and China, before continuing through Japan to Alaska. Canada was next in line, followed by a hop across the Atlantic to Portugal before returning home to Southampton via Spain and France. The 23,254-mile circuit would, they estimated, be completed in 293 hours of flying.

They had not got far when they encountered their first problem. In Civitavecchia, a seaport on the west coast of Italy, they collided with some floating driftwood and damaged the plane. Shortly afterwards, engine failure forced them to make a landing on a lake in Greece. A new engine was sent from England, but that failed over India, obliging them to land at Parlu, close to Jodhpur.

Another engine duly arrived, but the radiator broke and had to be replaced at Allahabad. Bad weather forced the team to land on Akyab Island, off the Burmese coast. Then, as they took off from Akyab Harbour, their airplane plunged into the water and was completely destroyed.

The dauntless trio awaited delivery of a new Vulture, and on 25 June they took to the air again. In Shanghai, Andrews, suffering from heatstroke, was replaced by another airman. He rejoined the crew after his recovery, at Kasumigaura naval base in Tokyo.

From there the men struggled along the barren Russian coast, out of radio contact with the rest of the world, buffeted by high winds and blinded by fog. Maclaren and Andrews became ill with fevers, and had to stop and rest until they had recovered. Leaving West Kamchatka on 4 August, almost five months after they had set off from Britain, they hit dense fog above Bering Island, between Russia and Alaska. Forced to land at sea, they not only survived, but miraculously succeeded in beaching their craft. They were rescued by a passing Russian ship.

It was a heroic end to a heroic British failure.

42

Arthur Pedrick:
Patently Having a Laugh

Deluded madman or canny satirist who subverted the patents process by exposing loopholes? Arthur Pedrick of Selsey, who filed 162 patents in the United Kingdom between 1962 and 1976, has supporters on both sides.

According to the inventor, his cat Ginger provided him with invaluable assistance in his work, and indeed many of the inventions for which he sought patents were aimed to make his pet's life a little easier. For instance, there was patent number GB1426698 – the 'Photon Push-Pull Radiation Detector for Use in Chromatically Selective Cat Flap Control'. The idea – one that would surely be welcomed by many cat owners – was that the cat flap would only permit cats of a certain colour to enter, keeping out unwanted visitors.

Among the other outlandish ideas Pedrick sent to be patented from his 'One-Man Photo-Electric Research Laboratories' (a.k.a. the 'One Man Think Tank Nuclear Fusion Research Laboratories') were:

'GB1121630: Controlling the spin of a golf ball, to prevent slicing or hooking or topspin. The ball has flaps which are normally held flush with the surface of the ball by magnets. If the ball has been mishit and is spinning, the centrifugal effect overcomes the magnetic force, and the flaps project as shown to reduce the spin. Additionally, the internal structure of the ball reflects radio waves from a homing device carried by the golfer, making it easier to find if it is lost in the rough.'

GB1453920: An 'Apparatus For Extinguishing Fires In High Rise Block Buildings Of Uniform Transverse Cross-Section Or Plan'. Fire curtains would be secured on the roofs of high-rise buildings and, in the event of fire, would be dropped to envelope the entire building. There would be openings at rooms where inhabitants would congregate.

GB1047735: 'Arrangements for the transfer of fresh water from one location on the earth's surface to another at a different latitude, for the purpose of irrigation, with pumping energy derived from the effect of the earth's rotation about the polar axis'. *In great detail and over pages of mathematical equations, Pedrick describes an idea for passing snow and ice from the Antarctic through pipes to irrigate the Australian outback, enabling the growth of crops and the feeding of the world. Pedrick suggests that the snow be compressed into hard balls that would be fired along the pipeline like bullets.*

41

A.E. Housman:
A Great Poet (but a Loser in Love)

According to his brother Lawrence, the poet Alfred Edward Housman was 'shy, proud, reserved, reticent, taciturn, staid, sardonic, secretive, undemonstrative, and glum'. To that list might be added the word 'repressed'. It was a common enough condition in Victorian times.

While he was a Classics student at Oxford, Housman fell hopelessly in love with another student: the handsome, athletic Moses Jackson. The poet would retain his passion for Jackson for the remainder of his life, and express it in many of his poems. But the heterosexual Jackson would never return those feelings. As Housman bluntly put it: 'There was no response in kind.'

Despite his exceptional intellect Housman failed his final exams, returning his papers mostly blank or defaced by random scribbles. It is thought that he suffered some kind of breakdown, precipitated in part by his unrequited love.

In 1882 he took a job at the London Patent Office, where Jackson also worked. He moved into a flat with Moses and his brother Adalbert, where he lived for four years, studying Greek and Latin in the evenings at the British Museum Library. When Moses married and took a job as a teacher in Karachi, Housman became a virtual recluse. At the same time, however, he began to gain a reputation as an expert on classical matters, and became a professor, first at University College London then at Cambridge.

When Adalbert died of typhoid, the loss of his closest friend prompted the distraught Housman to write *A Shropshire Lad*. It was rejected by several publishers, and in 1896 Housman was forced to pay for its printing himself. The collection has been in print ever since, and is one of the best-known and most popular depictions of a lost rural England.

Forty years after they had first met, Housman received news that Moses Jackson was dying of stomach cancer in Canada. He sent him a copy of *Last Poems*, the only book of poetry apart from *A Shropshire Lad* that he published in his lifetime.

It was the closest he ever came to writing a love letter.

'There was little about melancholy that he didn't know; there was little else that he did.'

W.H. AUDEN, POET, OF FELLOW POET, ALFRED, LORD TENNYSON

40

William Topaz McGonagall:
Not a Poet and Didn't Know It

God told this devout Christian to 'Write! Write!' and that's what
he did, with a superhuman, if wholly misplaced, dedication.
During his lifetime, McGonagall produced a vast body of what
could be loosely described as 'poetry'. It was notoriously bad, but
he seems to have had little concern for the opinions of others.

McGonagall was born in Edinburgh in 1825, but grew up in
Dundee, where he was apprenticed as a handloom weaver. In
1877, he discovered his true calling. He was seized with the desire
to write poetry.

In search of a patron, McGonagall applied straight to the top,
writing to Queen Victoria herself. A royal minion sent him a letter of rejection, which McGonagall inexplicably interpreted as
encouragement. He decided that the monarch should experience
his work first hand, and in July 1878 set out from Dundee to Bal-
moral on foot – a distance of sixty miles. Arriving soaking wet
from a thunderstorm he had encountered en route, he announced
himself as 'the Queen's Poet'. He was told that he could not be 'the
Queen's Poet' as that role was already occupied by Alfred, Lord
Tenyson, the Poet Laureate. McGonagall was sent packing.

His writing continued unabated. A strong enemy of drink, he
would recite his poetry and give speeches in pubs and taverns,
much to the ire of the publicans.

His most lucrative work was at a local circus, where he read his lyrics while the audience pelted him with eggs, flour, herrings, potatoes and stale bread. These events, which earned him 15 shillings a night, came to an end only when they became so rowdy that they were banned by magistrates.

With his large family suffering from his lack of earnings, some friends paid for the publication of a book – *Poetic Gems* – which kept him going for a while.

It was around this time that he gained a middle name, after receiving a letter from a hoaxer claiming to be 'King Thibaw Min of Burma'. With the letter, the 'king' knighted the poet 'Sir Topaz, Knight of the White Elephant of Burma'. From that day on, McGonagall styled himself thus.

William Topaz McGonagall died penniless in Edinburgh in 1902. He left behind such gems as these lines on the Tay Bridge Disaster:

'Beautiful Railway Bridge of the Silv'ry Tay!
Alas! I am very sorry to say
That ninety lives have been taken away
On the last Sabbath day of 1879,
Which will be remember'd for a very long time…
I must now conclude my lay
By telling the world fearlessly without the least dismay
That your central girders would not have given way,
At least many sensible men do say,
Had they been supported on each side with buttresses,
At least many sensible men confesses,
For the stronger we our houses do build,
The less chance we have of being killed.'

39

Clarence Charles Hatry:
The Serial Bankrupt Who May Have
Caused the Stock Market Crash of 1929

At one point he owned the largest yacht in Britain, a stable of thoroughbred racehorses, a Mayfair house complete with rooftop swimming pool, and his own in-house pub in the basement, which he had named 'Ye Old Stanhope Arms'.

From a lowly start as a West End clerk, Hatry rose to control the Commercial Bank of London. But in 1924 his bank failed to the tune of £5,000,000, forcing him to pawn his wife's jewellery, which was worth more than a million pounds, and borrow from friends in order to set up in business again.

Before long he had made his second fortune and was seated at the head of a vast business empire encompassing photographic supplies, cameras, vending machines and loan operations. In 1928 he set his sights on United Steel, responsible for ten percent of all the steel produced in Britain. However, having exhausted all his contacts at the Bank of England and in the City, he was unable to raise the requisite capital. It soon emerged that the success of his empire was a mirage. Far from being one of the wealthiest men in Britain, Hatry was up to his eyes in debt. Having been caught forging stock certificates and issuing unauthorised shares, he was forced to declare himself bankrupt for a second time, on 20 September 1929

Hatry's financial demise lost investors about £75 million, and caused the Dow Jones to drop by two per cent, so that many would hold him partially responsible for the crash that began nine days later, devastating financial markets and national economies around the world.

He was sentenced to fourteen years in prison, two with hard labour. In jail he assumed the role of librarian, and became keen on books. On his release in 1939 he entered the book trade, managing to build up a portfolio of twenty bookshops, two magazines, several publishing houses and a printing company.

Needless to say he went bankrupt again, for the third time, in the 1950s.

38

Leander Starr Jameson:
Leader of the Jameson Raid

Leander Starr Jameson, a Scottish doctor by profession, arrived in Southern Africa in search of diamonds. He left with his reputation in tatters, forever hitched to the disastrous escapade that bears his name.

As Administrator General of Matabeleland, Jameson was commissioned by Cecil Rhodes, Prime Minister of Cape Colony, to lead a force of around 600 men against Boer leader Paul Kruger's Transvaal Republic. It was hoped that the action would trigger an uprising by the mainly British expatriate workers in the region.

The expected uprising failed to materialise, leaving Jameson's force massively outnumbered by Transvaal troops. On 2 January 1896 he was taken prisoner and handed over to the British authorities. Back at home, he was initially charged with treason and sentenced to death, but was reprieved, serving only four months of a fifteen-month sentence. Badly timed, politically disastrous and quixotic to the point of suicidal, the Jameson Raid is generally held to have sparked the Boer War, and spelt the end of Rhodes' domination of South African politics.

Jameson, who must have had an attractive side to his character (he inspired Kipling's poem *If*) was officially rehabilitated, and ended up in Rhodes' old job as Prime Minister of Cape Colony. He died in London in 1917, loaded with honours, but remembered above all for the military misadventure that started a war.

37

Bunglers in Benghazi:
Who Dares... Loses

Once upon a time the British Foreign Secretary would have looked up from his *digestif* at the Carlton Club and briefly interrupted his companion's anecdote to dispatch a gunboat that would show Johnny Foreigner who was boss. 'Gunboat diplomacy' was what they aptly called it, and it worked – then.

Yet to judge from an incident at the beginning of March 2011, we still believe we are a force to be reckoned with. As Libya teetered on the brink of civil war, the British government without warning applied its default solution to a sticky situation – it sent in the SAS. Under cover of darkness, eight of our finest – six SAS troops, an MI6 agent and a translator – were dropped into Libya by helicopter.

Almost as soon as their boots touched Libyan soil, they were surrounded by a group of farmers – sorry, crack rebel fighters – opposed to Gaddafi. The rebels believed them to be foreign mercenaries, a suspicion that may have been provoked by the fact that they were carrying weapons, reconnaissance equipment and espionage gear, and had multiple passports in their pockets. Their mission? To 'keep an eye on the humanitarian situation in Benghazi' and to hand over a personal letter to the rebel leaders from British PM, David Cameron (who was emulating a tactic that had often been used by his hero, Margaret Thatcher).

It was all dreadfully embarrassing. A tape was played on Libyan

State TV in which a man alleged to be the British ambassador could be heard begging a rebel operative for clemency. In the end, the group was unceremoniously kicked out of Libya, while back home coalition leaders passed the blame parcel until the music stopped at the very moment that Foreign Secretary William Hague was grasping it in his sweaty hands. Hague bravely got to his feet in Parliament and, grimacing, admitted that he had personally sanctioned the ill-fated mission.

*

We should have known better. Libya has never been a happy hunting ground for the SAS, and Benghazi itself was the scene of two memorable bunglings during the Second World War. Both involved the unit's doughty founder, David Stirling.

On 25 March 1942 seven SAS troops, including Stirling himself, made their way to Benghazi to blow up Italian warships at anchor in the city's harbour. Armed with a sack of limpet mines and an ingenious folding canoe, they prepared to carry out their mission. There was just one problem – the canoe was terrific at folding and being portable, but it did not do the other vital thing required of it – float.

Mission aborted.

But Stirling was not a man to give up easily. In order to push through his idea of creating the SAS, he had smuggled himself into Middle East HQ in Cairo and, despite being on crutches due to a broken leg, climbed a high wall to present his brainchild to Commander-in-Chief General Claude Auchinleck.

Just a couple of months after the debacle of the first attack, this model of British fortitude and perseverance was back in Benghazi, this time with two rubber dinghies. On a beach near the city, he and his men tried to inflate the dinghies, but soon found themselves undergoing a familiar experience. The dinghies had holes in them – and there was no bicycle repair kit to hand.

Mission aborted. Again.

SOME OTHER MILITARY MISADVENTURES

The Battle of Watling Street, 60 or 61 BC

A British force estimated at anywhere between 100,000 and 230,000 allowed itself to be channelled into a narrow gorge by the wily Roman Governor of Great Britain, Gaius Suetonius Paulinus. The Britons, led by the Queen of the Iceni tribe, Boudica, were routed by Suetonius's 10,000 men. Only 400 Romans are said to have died, while Boudica lost upwards of 80,000 men and is said to have committed suicide shortly after.

Battle of Stirling Bridge, September 11, 1297

English military commander John de Warenne, 7th Earl of Surrey, had trounced the Scots at Dunbar the previous year, and thought the rematch at Stirling Bridge was just a matter of turning up. Anxious to avoid any unnecessary wastage of time or money, he and his fellow commander, Hugh de Cressingham, decided against travelling upstream to cross the River Forth at a wide ford, choosing instead to cross at a bridge so narrow that only two horsemen could pass over it at one time. Once around 5,000 English troops had crossed the bridge, the Scottish leader William Wallace ordered the attack. His unarmoured, lightly armed troops divided the enemy army in two and inflicted an unexpected defeat on the English.

Afghanistan, 1838, 1878, 2001...

Why do we bother? Afghanistan is the British army's bogey team. Twice in the nineteenth century we invaded Afghanistan from India, during the First Afghan War of 1838 to 1842 and then in the second instalment of the same conflict from 1878 to 1880. The objective was to keep the Russians out of the region and to bring local tribal leaders into line. The first invasion ended in one of the worst defeats ever inflicted on the British Empire, and while the second brought a little more success, the British authorities soon learned that defeating the Afghans was not the same thing as controlling them. *Plus ça change*.

Gallipoli

Not long into the First World War, which was, of course, not short on military cock-ups, Winston Churchill dreamed up the Gallipoli campaign, a plan to end the war early by opening a new eastern front. The attack on Turkish positions in the Dardanelles was launched on 19 February 1915. By the time Allied troops evacuated in December that year, having failed to defeat the Turks, 44,000 Allied troops and more than 86,000 Turkish troops were dead.

The Fall of Singapore

The loss of this supposedly impregnable fortress in February 1942 to two Japanese divisions – estimated to be just a third of the defending force – represented the largest ever surrender of British-led troops.

36

Devon Loch:
Defeat from the Jaws of Victory

As dawn broke on the day of the 1956 Grand National, many punters thought Devon Loch, ridden by future bestselling writer Dick Francis, was in with a good chance. A couple of wins at Cheltenham, plus the fact that he was owned by the Queen Mother, had tempted many to put their money on him.

There was drama from the off, as favourites Must and Early Mist fell at the first fence, leaving M'as-tu-vu in the lead and Devon Loch running along comfortably in the middle of the field. By the end of the first circuit, Francis had had to deal with only one problem, when a horse fell immediately in front of him: steering his mount adroitly around obstacle, he galloped on unscathed.

Towards the end of the race, things were still going well. Devon Loch was moving along easily, and Francis noted cheerfully that the other jockeys were having to work harder than he was to cajole their horses over the final fences.

Safely over the last, the remaining horses faced the Elbow – Aintree's long, punishing run to the finishing post. Francis was now in the lead, and confident that the race was in his pocket. 'Never had I felt such power in reserve, such confidence in my mount, such calm in my mind,' he wrote later. The crowd rose as one, cheering what they had no doubt was going to be a royal winner.

Seventy yards from the line… sixty yards… fifty… Then, all of a sudden, Devon Loch did an extraordinary thing. He seemed to jump, as if there was a fence in front of him – yet there was no fence. For a split second, he resembled a galloping horse in a 17th-century painting – front legs stretched out before him, hind legs behind him – before he collapsed awkwardly onto his stomach. The crowd issued a collective groan as the animal climbed unsteadily to his feet, Francis desperately trying to restart him as first ESB (the eventual winner) and then all the other horses staggered past him. Devon Loch did not rejoin the race. He just stood there, looking embarrassed.

A number of theories were put forward to explain this bizarre incident. One was that the shadow of the water jump, the last fence on the first circuit, stretched across the course and the horse thought it was a fence. A policeman advanced the similar theory that Devon Loch might have mistaken a dark, damp patch on the course for a fence. It was also suggested that cramp in his hindquarters could have been the cause. Francis himself was convinced that the huge roar of the crowd, as they cheered a royal winner to the rafters, was responsible.

The Queen Mother was characteristically sanguine. 'Oh, that's racing!' she said. God bless 'er.

'I see no particular objection to giving women a chance to ride in races now and again... Such races should be on the Flat and be placed last on the card so that those racegoers not interested can return home for tea and Magic Roundabout.'

ROGER MORTIMER, JOURNALIST

35

Jabez Balfour:
The Rise and Precipitous Fall of the 'Great Liberator'

Jabez Spencer Balfour came from nowhere and it was to nowhere that he returned.

The Liberator Building Society, founded by Balfour in 1868, sported the motto 'Libera sedes liberum facit' ('A free home makes a free man'). In 1871, the Liberator's assets were £70,000; by 1875, they amounted to £500,000. By 1879, it had overtaken the Leeds Permanent to become Britain's biggest building society. Balfour became known fondly by investors as 'the Great Liberator' – the man who had helped millions of ordinary people buy their own home.

Such wealth also brought large homes for Balfour himself, and a champagne lifestyle. He entered politics and was elected as a Liberal MP for Tamworth in 1880, and in 1889 became MP for Burnley.

By this time his business had grown into a veritable empire, incorporating construction, transport and mining companies, as well as a bank – the London and General. It was, however, all built on an illusion. Balfour was moving assets between his companies at prices greater than they were worth, thereby enabling him to declare vast profits and pay himself and his fellow directors handsome annual dividends. Just over a century later the same type of scam would be repeated by Enron and rogue US businessman Bernie Madoff.

Balfour's scheme began to unravel when a downswing in the country's economy began to put pressure on the Liberator. By 1892 the *Financial Times* and the *Economist* were beginning to ask questions about the business. The resulting lack of confidence led to a run on the London and General bank, the last run on a British bank until Northern Rock in 2007.

The Liberator collapsed with combined debts of £7 million (about £500 million in today's terms). Thousands lost their life savings and several elderly ladies died of shock on learning they were ruined. Large numbers of working men who had invested everything they had in the building society killed themselves.

Balfour resigned immediately as an MP, purportedly to work on a rescue plan for the business. In reality, however, he was working on his own escape.

The authorities issued an arrest warrant, but by the time they started looking for him he was far away, ensconced in a suburb of Buenos Aires with the two young daughters of a former business associate. To the outside world he presented Ethel Sophie and Lucia Maria Freeman as his wards, but in reality he was living scandalously with them in a *ménage à trois*.

He had chosen Argentina because he believed there was no extradition treaty between it and Britain. As soon as he found out that a newly agreed treaty was awaiting signature, he fled in panic to the small town of Salta, on the Chilean border.

Fortuitously discovering that you could not be extradited if you were involved in litigation, Balfour then bribed various people in Salta to sue him. Again and again, just as the Buenos Aires authorities were on the point of issuing an extradition order, proceedings against him would be launched, and the authorities would be foiled.

Chief Inspector Frank Froest, one of Scotland Yard's finest, was despatched to bring Balfour back at any cost. Froest, later instrumental in the capture of the notorious murderer Dr. Crippen, travelled to Salta, where he simply kidnapped the fugitive financier, having chartered a train specially for the purpose getting him to Buenos Aires. The local authorities at Salta, seeing a lucrative source of income vanishing into the distance, sent a posse after the train, but when one of the men on horseback stood on the tracks in front of the approaching locomotive, waving a warrant for Balfour's release, the resolute British detective ordered the train driver to carry on. Horse and rider were were both killed. In Buenos Aires, Froest smuggled his captive onto the steamship *Tartar Prince*. At last Balfour was on his way back to Britain.

It took the jury 35 minutes to find him guilty at his trial. Recalling the thousands of lives Balfour had ruined, the judge showed him no mercy, sentencing him to fourteen years with hard labour. He did his time in Wormwood Scrubs, Parkhurst, Portland and Pentonville prisons, before being released on 13 April 1906, having earned three years' remission for good behaviour.

On his release he was whisked away, like an expelled *Big Brother* competitor, by Lord Northcliffe, the newspaper magnate. His memoir *My Prison Years* became an instant bestseller and received a twenty-six-week serialisation in the *Weekly Dispatch*.

Jabez Balfour lived off his book and serial earnings, while also working as a mining consultant, first in Burma and then in South Wales. In 1916 the greatest financial fraudster in British history died of a heart attack on the London to Fishguard Express.

34

John Stonehouse:
The Disappearing Man

John Stonehouse had just two ambitions: to be Prime Minister and to be a millionaire.

He became a Labour MP in a by-election in 1957, and considered it only a matter of time before he shimmied up the greasy pole of Whitehall politics all the way to the top. His arrogance made him unpopular with everyone except the press, who prized him as a source of entertaining headlines. He was handsome and charismatic, and something of a ladies' man, with an eye for the younger female party workers.

In government, Stonehouse served as Junior Aviation Minister and Minister of State for Technology before Prime Minister Harold Wilson gave him the job of Postmaster General and then Minister of Posts and Telecommunications. It was rumoured that Wilson had promoted him only in the hope that he would mess up, thereby permitting him to get rid of the arrogant sod once and for all. In the end the country got rid of Wilson instead, in the 1970 general election, whereupon Wilson showed his dislike of Stonehouse by not even offering him a post in the Shadow Cabinet.

The loss of his ministerial salary and the simultaneous fading of his political ambitions were a double blow to Stonehouse. The only way forward was to focus on the second of his ambitions. He set himself a target of seven years to make his first million.

He launched a number of companies, but business was not his strong suit, and by 1974 he was in serious trouble. He resorted to falsifying his companies' accounts, which before long attracted the attention of the Department of Trade, who launched an investigation into his affairs. The *Sunday Times* 'Insight' team began to sniff around, sensing a juicy scandal.

Stonehouse decided there was only one way out.

On 20 November 1974, a pile of clothes was discovered on a beach in Miami. When it was ascertained that they belonged to the former minister, the papers reported his sad demise by his own hand. Obituaries appeared, a minute's silence was held in the House of Commons, and his wife and children mourned his passing.

Yet Stonehouse was far from dead. In fact, he was *en route* for Australia, communicating all the while with his secretary, raven-haired beauty Sheila Buckley, with whom he had been conducting an affair for some time. Prior to leaving London, he had plundered his ailing companies, and had set up bank accounts in a number of countries.

Meanwhile, back in Miami, his body had puzzlingly failed to be washed ashore, and the FBI began to wonder if the former Postmaster General had been the victim of a Mafia contract killing. MI5, meanwhile, were following another line of enquiry, believing that he was a Soviet spy who had been spirited back to Russia. The *News of the World* plumped for a more succinct explanation, running the headline: 'SHARKS ATE JOHN STONEHOUSE'.

Shortly after arriving in Australia, having island-hopped through the Pacific, Stonehouse became the victim of a bizarre coincidence. Melbourne police had been asked to look out for Lord Lucan, the English aristocrat who had recently disappeared after killing his children's nanny. One day, a bank teller became suspicious of the way a customer had been juggling his accounts and, mindful of fraud and money-laundering, passed his suspicions to the police. The man was John Stonehouse, and the police began to keep tabs on him. Since he was English and roughly the same build as Lucan, they drew the inevitable conclusion that he and the fugitive aristo were one and the same.

On Christmas Eve 1974, the authorities made their move. They arrested Stonehouse at his home, convinced they had nabbed Lord Lucan. However, Stonehouse immediately confessed his real identity, as well as his many misdeeds, and after six months of legal shenanigans he was deported back to England. Incredibly, he was released on bail. Even more astonishingly, he refused to resign his parliamentary seat, brazenly taking Sheila to tea in the House of Commons, and even attending the Labour Party Conference, where he was loudly booed.

Eventually, in the summer of 1976, following a 67-day trial – at the time the longest fraud trial in British legal history – Stonehouse was found guilty of 21 charges of fraud and theft, totalling around £150,000, and was sent to prison for seven years.

John Stonehouse walked out of the gates of his prison after three years, welcomed by only person who had remained loyal to him – Sheila Buckley. They married and had a child, and he turned to writing books for a living. He died of a heart attack in 1988.

'It will be years - not in my time - before a woman will become Prime Minister.'

MARGARET THATCHER, 1974

33

Horatio Bottomley:
Fraudster, Bankrupt and
Member of Parliament

As the chaplain of Wormwood Scrubs was making his rounds one day, he came upon an inmate hunched over a mailbag. 'Ah, Bottomley! Sewing?' asked the chaplain. 'No, reaping,' replied Horatio Bottomley, fraudster, bankrupt and former MP for the constituencies of Islington North and Hackney South.

Bottomley's life was colourful, to say the least. Born in the East End in 1860, he grew up in an orphanage in Birmingham, then worked as a legal shorthand writer and court reporter. In the process he gained an intimate knowledge of the law, put to good use later in life on the many occasions when he was obliged to defend himself in court.

It first came in handy in 1885, when he had to defend his own printing and publishing firm, from which large amounts of money had gone missing, in a bankruptcy case.

Bottomley devoted a large portion of his ingenuity and his career to separating people from their money. His honey-voiced persuasion worked on members of the public, judges and beddable women alike. He even founded the *Financial Times* in January 1888 to talk up his projects and give them a veneer of respectability. In 1908 he was charged with conspiracy to defraud, but the jury was unable to reach a verdict, partly because of the chaos of Bottomley's financial record-keeping. Though in 1906 he had successfully bought his way into Parliament, he was thrown out six years later when he was declared bankrupt – a process to which he was no stranger, having been served with as many as 67 bankruptcy petitions between 1901 and 1905.

His next publishing venture, launched in 1906, was the tub-thumpingly patriotic periodical *John Bull*, which built up a circulation of a million. The magazine's popularity during World War One made its owner well-known throughout the country. In 1918 he stormed back in to Parliament as an independent candidate, and a year later founded his own political party, the People's League, hoping to establish a third political force in the country that would be for neither labour nor capital. Meanwhile his court appearances in libel and other cases – some of which were clever ruses concocted by Bottomley himself to deflect attention from his various financial scams – became legendary, especially as he invariably defended himself. One judge thought he had performed so well that he offered him his wig during the case.

In the end it was his John Bull Victory Bond Club that brought him down. A scheme to enable small savers to lend money to the government, it resembled Premium Bonds, except that winners received prizes rather than cash. When the mismanaged scheme went under in 1921, Bottomley was charged with fraud, perjury and false accounting. In 1922 he was sentenced to seven years in prison and, unsurprisingly, once again lost his seat in Parliament.

Released from prison in 1927, he spent his last years performing a sad one-man show about himself in music halls. He died penniless in 1933.

32=

Lambert Simnel and Perkin Warbeck:
Strange Imposters

They may sound like anagrams of real names, but Lambert Simnel and Perkin Warbeck were two real, if bizarre, pretenders to the throne of King Henry VII during the turbulent latter part of the fifteenth century.

Lambert Simnel

Lambert Simnel was born around 1477. His origins are obscure: his father is variously claimed to have been a baker, a tradesman and an organ-maker. What is certain is that around the age of ten, he became the pupil of an Oxford-trained priest, Roger Simon, who on remarking the boy's resemblance to the 'Princes in the Tower', Edward V of England and his brother, Richard of Shrewsbury, 1st Duke of York, dreamed up a fantastic hustle.

Simon's ruse was to teach Simnel courtly etiquette and present him as the younger of the two princes, Richard of York, in order to challenge the legitimacy of Henry VII, who had succeeded Richard III after defeating him in battle in 1485.

The scheming priest changed tack, however, when he heard a rumour that the Earl of Warwick, a nephew of Edward IV, had also died in the Tower. The Earl and Simnel were both about ten years old, so it would be easier to pass him off as Warwick than the Princes, who were both much older. Simon's new story was that 'Warwick' had escaped from the Tower and had come into his care.

He took his protegé to Ireland, where the King's enemy the Earl of Kildare declared his willingness to support the claim and invade England (any excuse would have done). On 24 May 1487 Simnel was crowned 'King Edward VI' in Dublin, whereupon Kildare began to assemble an army to oust King Henry.

King Henry must have been rather bemused, since he knew that Warwick was alive and well (if locked up in the Tower). To prove it, he paraded the boy in the streets of London.

This did not stop yet another earl, the Earl of Lincoln, who had once been Richard III's rightful successor, from joining the conspiracy. He told Warwick's sister Margaret, now wife of the Duke of Burgundy, that he had helped the young prince escape from the Tower, and Margaret promptly raised an army of 2,000 Flemish mercenaries, sending them to Ireland to join the fun.

In early June 1487, Lambert Simnel, a ten-year-old nobody with the airs and graces of a king, landed on the Lancashire coast at the head of an army of Flemish and Irish troops. They faced the King's army on 16 June at the Battle of Stoke Field and lost resoundingly. Most of the leaders were captured or killed. Simon was spared only because he was a man of God, but spent the rest of his days in prison.

Lambert Simnel himself was pardoned by King Henry (as a child, he was deemed not responsible for his actions) and spent the remainder of his life working as a spit-turner in the royal kitchen.

Perkin Warbeck

Perkin Warbeck was born in Tournai in Belgium around 1474, the son of John de Werbeque, a French official. Claiming to be the Duke of York, the younger of the 'Princes in the Tower', he was a far more active pretender than Simnel.

Warbeck launched his campaign to become King of England at the court of Burgundy in 1490; then, having learned the ruse from Simnel, he headed for Ireland to raise support. This time, however, even the Irish were not inclined to help and Warbeck was forced to return to France, where he was championed by the French king Charles VIII and Edward IV's sister, Margaret (who seems to have been up for anything, having raised an army for Simnel four years earlier). She even claimed to recognise Warbeck as her nephew.

Warbeck continued to be fêted in foreign courts. In 1493, he attended the funeral of Frederick III, the Holy Roman Emperor, and was welcomed there as King Richard IV of England by the new emperor Maximilian I.

In July 1495, he gathered a small army and attempted to land at Deal in Kent for a fresh attempt at the throne. Before he could even get off his boat, 150 of his troops were killed and Warbeck was forced to retreat to Ireland. There he enjoyed a slightly warmer reception than the previous time, and he joined with the Earl of Desmond to lay siege to Waterford. When the Loyalist town proved too resistant, Warbeck moved on again, this time to Scotland. The Scots were, of course, more than happy to annoy the English in any way they could, and Warbeck received a particularly warm welcome from James IV, who even allowed him to marry his cousin.

In September 1496, with James' financial help, Warbeck mounted another invasion of England. It was again unsuccessful, as he had no support from the borders, and James IV finally got bored with him, expelling him from his kingdom. Warbeck returned to Ireland and tried once again to capture Waterford (clearly an *idée fixe* with him). Once again, he failed.

The man could not be faulted for perseverance. In 1497, he landed in Cornwall, hoping to capitalise upon the mood of rebellion that had persisted there since the unsuccessful Cornish uprising against the King earlier that year. He managed to gather a new 6,000-strong army, who pronounced him 'King Richard IV' on Bodmin Moor, and started a march towards London. But in Devon Warbeck heard that the King's army was not far away, and deserted his men, hiding in an abbey in Hampshire until being captured a few days later and imprisoned in the Tower.

There Warbeck met a genuine claimant to the throne, the Earl of Warwick (still alive, still well, and still locked up in the Tower). The pair made a joint escape attempt in 1499, but were captured. As a foreigner Warbeck could not be tried for treason and had thus far escaped execution. But his luck had finally run out. On 23 November 1499 Perkin Warbeck, a chancer if ever there was one, was hanged at Tyburn.

A LOT OF LOTTERY LOSERS

No, not us poor saps who religiously spend our pound twice a week but win zilch. Rather, the people who win big and lose bigger.

Mukhtar Mohidin

In 1994 Mohidin, a Blackburn factory worker, became the lottery's first multi-millionaire when he won £17.9 million. It gave him nothing but trouble. First he fled the country, then his family fought over the money. His wife left him, and a friend claimed that he had provided money for the winning ticket and was entitled to a share of the prize. When Mohidin's family (themselves squabbling over the money) told the friend to drop his claim, the situation in the area became so volatile that authorities feared it would turn into a riot. Even charitable deeds turned sour; when Mohidin donated £300,000 for an Islamic community centre in Blackburn, the building was left unfinished and decaying when the local Muslims refused to use a place that had been funded by gambling.

Robbie Woods

When this 24-year-old garage mechanic won £1.3 million, he became an instant target for gold-diggers. Perhaps this isn't surprising given his wealth-flaunting behaviour: he had a High Court injunction served on him to stop the noise of what was described as a 'six-month jacuzzi party', and boasted to council officials that he was so rich he could pay any fine they slapped on him.

Lee Ryan

Four months after he won £6.5 million in 1995, the East Midlands' first lottery millionaire was jailed for eighteen months for handling stolen cars. Although he bought a £2 million mansion and helicopter, Ryan declared that winning the lottery was the worst thing that could have happened to him: 'After winning and seeing how people are with money and seeing how they chase it and adore it, it's just made me shallow. I felt unclean and tainted by it all.' His marriage collapsed and he was charged with drink-driving. Ten years after his win, Ryan was reported to be living in a small flat in Kyrgyzstan. By 2010, the last of his money had gone after risky property investments went belly-up in the turmoil of the troubled former Soviet republic.

Iorworth Hoare

Following a string of convictions for sexual offences, Iorworth Hoare was imprisoned for life in 1989 for the attempted rape of a 59-year-old woman identified only as 'Mrs A'. On day release in 2004, he purchased a lottery ticket and won £7 million. Mrs A., who had received only £5,000 from the Criminal Injuries Compensation Board, tried to sue Hoare for damages for her psychological injuries, In January 2008, even though the six-year statute of limitations had long expired, the Law Lords changed the law to allow him to be sued, and in 2009 he agreed to pay the woman, 79 at the time, £100,000.

30

Keith Brown, Ken Evans and the 1993 Grand National: A National Embarrassment

It was a miserable day. Rain had been falling on Aintree race-course since dawn. Spectators, horses and jockeys were all drenched. By the time the starter, bowler-hatted Captain Keith Brown, climbed up onto the starter's podium, everyone's patience was wearing thin.

But just as the horses at last came into line and the start seemed imminent, a group of animal rights protesters ran onto the track. The increasingly jittery steeds were sent back to the paddock to trudge round and round in the mud.

It took the police ten minutes to clear the course, whereupon Captain Brown again ushered the horses towards the white starting tape that hung loosely across the rain-sodden course. By this time several of the horses had had enough. Chatham stubbornly refused to move and Royal Speedmaster was performing nervous pirouettes. Still, this was the moment when Brown should have cast his rule-book pedantry to the wind and let them go. He didn't. Instead, the horses were made to wait for an age until the miscreants had been shoved into something approaching a line.

When Brown did finally pull down on the start lever, disaster struck. The starting tape caught on the chin of a horse named Direct, and trailed behind the departing animals. The Captain raised the red flag to signal a false start. The 'recall man', Ken Evans, waved *his* flag further down the track. And the horses were sent back to the start.

By this time the crowd was in as much of a lather as the animals they had put their money on. Again Captain Brown pushed down on the lever; again the horses leapt forward. And again the tape became caught up in the melee, this time wrapping itself somewhat dangerously around the neck of jockey Richard Dunwoody. The starter raised his flag to signal another false start, but it failed to unfurl, so that further down the track Evans failed to raise his flag at all. Thirty horses thundered past him and jumped the first fence. Then they jumped the second, and the third – with the nine riders who had spotted the recall left bemused at the start.

Farce ensued. Red-faced men in smart coats and brown trilbies waved flags futilely at the horses, but the jockeys mistook them for protesters and galloped on. A couple of traffic cones were positioned at the famous Chair fence but, unsurprisingly, were ignored by the racing horses. The crowd, infuriated by the ridiculous spectacle unfolding in front of them, booed as the horses passed them, and some riders, sensing at last that all was not well, pulled up.

Esha's Ness, a 50 to 1 shot, trained by Jenny Pitman and ridden by the unfortunate John White, jumped into the lead at the final fence, and galloped home to a hollow victory.

In the recriminations that followed, Captain Brown and Ken Evans took the flak for the 'race that never was', with Brown dubbed 'Captain Cockup' by the media.

To amateur jockey Jim Old: 'If Jesus Christ rode his flaming donkey like you just rode that horse, then he deserved to be crucified.'

FRED RIMELL, TRAINER

29

William Paterson and the Darien Scheme: Scotland's Last Tilt at the Big Time

Dreamed up by financial wizard William Paterson, the Scottish founder of the Bank of England, the Darien Scheme of the late 1690s was Scotland's last tilt at the big time – a desperate effort to break into the premier league with the English, Spanish and Dutch, after decades of war, famine and mismanagement had ruined the country's economy.

Scotland had fallen behind its bigger neighbour. Its navy was small and its trade with the rest of Europe poor, largely because it produced almost nothing that anyone else wanted. The Scottish Parliament decided that the only solution was to find ways to trade with Africa and the Indies, establishing a body called the Company of Scotland for the purpose. Money was to come from public subscription – and how they subscribed! Almost everyone with a spare fiver invested in the scheme, and £400,000 – roughly a third of the total wealth of the nation – poured into the Company's coffers from rich and poor alike.

Paterson's plan was to create a colony on the Isthmus of Panama. Instead of ships having to make the perilous voyage around Cape Horn to access the lucrative Pacific markets, they would unload their goods at the bay of Darien on Panama's Atlantic coast, from where they would be transported overland to the Pacific coast, to be loaded onto ships for their onward journey. It seemed a brilliant idea, and indeed anticipated the Panama Canal by several centuries.

On 14 July 1698, five ships – *Endeavour, Saint Andrew, Dolphin, Caledonia* and *Unicorn* – sailed out of Leith. There had been no shortage of volunteers to embark on the expedition, and the 1,200 people on board included famine-hit Highlanders and soldiers who had been discharged following the massacre at Glencoe. Only Paterson and Captain Robert Pennecuick, in overall command, knew the ultimate destination; the others found out from sealed envelopes that could only be opened once they were at sea. Fourteen weeks later, they arrived at Darien, which they promptly renamed 'New Caledonia'.

There they built Fort St. Andrew, a stronghold defended by fifty cannons. Land was cleared for the cultivation of crops and efforts were made to befriend the local natives. The locals, however, were not very interested in the trinkets the settlers had brought – items such as mirrors, combs and wigs that were altogether useless to them.

The spring of 1699 was a washout. Torrential rain and oppressive heat brought disease, and by March more than two hundred settlers had lost their lives. The death rate rose to ten a day and conditions became unbearable. The settlement's crops failed, and since the English colonies in America were forbidden by the king to trade with the Scots, supplies ran low. In July 1699, debilitated and fearing that the Spanish were about to invade, the survivors abandoned New Caledonia. Of the original 1,200, only 300 made it back to Scotland.

As it happened, a second expedition had already set out just before the survivors came home, arriving at New Caledonia in November 1699. They rebuilt the colony, and were persuaded to attack the Spanish, who were massing nearby. Although the attack was successful, it served only to galvanise their enemy. Fort St. Andrew was besieged and forced to surrender in March 1700. The beleaguered settlers were permitted to leave, but a mere handful managed to get back to Scotland.

The Darien failure was a defining moment in Scottish history. Not only did the Company of Scotland lose almost quarter of a million pounds, a huge sum in those days, but the country's pride took a near-fatal dent, as it finally became clear that Scotland would never be a world power in its own right.

As for William Paterson, he accompanied the settlers to Darien, where his wife and child died and he himself became seriously ill. He recovered, however, and returned to Scotland, where he campaigned vigorously for the Union between Scotland and England that eventually came to pass in 1707.

In the Acts of Union, England agreed to pay off Scotland's debts of £398,000, most of which had been notched up by the Company of Scotland.

And when the dust had settled, everybody swore that never again would a great Scottish company rise to world prominence only to come crashing down, bringing shame upon the prestige of a nation and its trusted financial institutions. *Never…*

28

Sir Fred Goodwin:
Royal Scottish *anker

After the banking crisis that almost brought civilization to its knees in October 2008, Royal Bank of Scotland's disgraced CEO Fred Goodwin was reported to be leaving RBS with a pension worth no less than £16 million. Many assumed Sir Fred would be speedily stripped both of his knighthood and his pension – not to mention his beloved vintage cars.

Fat chance.

It turned out you could screw up on a major scale, lose the country and individuals almost unimaginable sums of money, and still live out your days in vintage-upholstered luxury.

The question is therefore begged – should Sir Fred be included in this book? Or, fair reader, are the real losers you and I?

27

Jeremy Thorpe:
An Everyday Story of Conspiracy,
Obfuscation and 'Pillow-Biting'

May 1979 started very badly for Jeremy Thorpe, the dapper and urbane leader of the Liberal Party. In the general election on 3 May, he lost the North Devon Parliamentary seat he had held for twenty years. Five days later, he walked into the Old Bailey's Number One Court to face charges of attempted murder and conspiracy to murder, in what newspaper headlines billed as the 'Trial of the Century'.

How had this likeable and charismatic politician got himself embroiled in such sordid events?

Jeremy Thorpe had become leader of his party in 1967, following a career as a television interviewer and a barrister. He brought a new youthfulness and vigour to the Liberals, although at times he was accused of being gimmicky. Renowned for his Edwardian suits, silk waistcoats and jaunty trilbies, he began to taste success after the 1974 election, which resulted in a hung parliament. It seemed that the Liberals, with their 14 seats, would hold the balance of power and enter government for the first time since they were part of the War Cabinet during the Second World War. However, Thorpe declined Edward Heath's offer of a coalition and the post of Home Secretary, and in the next election Labour managed to secure a small majority.

Meanwhile, a cloud hung over Jeremy Thorpe's private life. In 1961 he had met former male model, Norman Scott, who was working as a stable lad. Scott alleged that he and Thorpe had a homosexual affair – allegations that came to the disapproving ears of Liberal Party leaders.

In 1975 things began to get more serious. A former airline pilot, Andrew Newton, ambushed Norman Scott while he walked his Great Dane, Rinka, on Exmoor. Armed with a gun, Newton shot the dog, before turning the barrel on Scott. Fortunately the weapon failed to go off and Scott was spared. In 1976, when Newton was tried for the incident, Scott took the opportunity to repeat his claim that he'd had an affair with Thorpe, alleging that Thorpe had threatened to kill him if he made their affair public. At the same time, Scott sold some love letters written to him by Thorpe, one of which was seized on with particular glee by the tabloids. In it Thorpe had written: 'Bunnies can and will go to France'. 'Bunnies' was Thorpe's pet name for Scott, and the sentence was meant to reassure him that he would be found a well-paid job in France. Newton was convicted, but the scandal also found a victim in Jeremy Thorpe, who was forced to resign.

But that was not the end of the matter.

When Newton was released from prison in 1977, he began to stir things up, claiming that he had been hired to kill Scott. On 4 August, it was reported that Thorpe, along with David Holmes, Deputy Treasurer of the Liberal Party, night club owner George Deakin, and businessman John Le Mesurier (*not* the actor who played Corporal Wilson in *Dad's Army*) had been arrested.

The peculiar trial was lambasted by satirists and magazines such as *Private Eye*. Peter Bessell, a former Liberal MP and a failed businessman, testified, in exchange for immunity from prosecution, that he had been present at a meeting when the murder of Norman Scott had been discussed. When it transpired that he had sold his story to the *Sunday Telegraph* for £25,000, and that this figure would be doubled if Thorpe were convicted, his credibility came into question. George Carmen QC, Thorpe's counsel, conceded that his client had been friends with Scott, but denied that there had been a sexual relationship. He claimed that Scott had been trying to blackmail the politician, and that and he and his associates had merely discussed ways they could frighten him off. Scott, meanwhile, described to a rapt courtroom his reluctant participation in homosexual activity: 'I just bit the pillow. I tried not to scream because I was frightened of waking Mrs Thorpe.'

Judge, Mr. Justice Cantley delivered an outrageously biased summing-up, describing Scott as 'a crook, an accomplished liar… a fraud'. On 22 June 1979, all four defendants were found not guilty and acquitted.

Yet cruel fate had not finished with Jeremy Thorpe. Shortly after his acquittal, he was found to be suffering from Parkinson's disease, and he never returned to the political stage.

'There was no impropriety whatsoever in my acquaintanceship with Miss Keeler.'

JOHN PROFUMO, BRITISH SECRETARY OF STATE FOR WAR
IN A COMMONS STATEMENT ABOUT CALL-GIRL CHRISTINE KEE-
LER. A FEW MONTHS LATER, HE ADMITTED THAT HE HAD LIED TO
THE HOUSE AND RESIGNED

26

The Great Auk: Eggstinct

Nineteenth century egg-collectors argued that their pastime was a scientific pursuit, but they were talking *guano*. Some were driven by the mysterious, irrational obsession that afflicts all collectors; others, more practical, by the colossal sums of money rare eggs could fetch on the market. Either way, the contribution to science was negligible.

One of the principal targets of these 'eggomaniacs' was the Great Auk, a lovable, flightless, penguin-like seabird native to Britain. Though awkward on land, it was a strong, graceful swimmer. The Great Auk was nigh irresistible to egg-collectors, since it laid only one egg each year. It was also in great demand for its down, fat and meat. The rarer it became, the more it was hunted.

In 1844, the last known pair of Great Auks was killed by fishermen on the Icelandic island of Eldey.

OTHER EXTINCT BRITISH MAMMALS, BIRDS AND FISH

10000 BC

The Arctic fox

Having evolved to survive extreme nippiness, the Arctic fox was no longer at home in balmy Britain once the Ice Age was over .

8000 BC

The Arctic lemming

Another victim of climate change. Britain became too warm for the Arctic lemming some 10,000 years ago, and the last specimens were seen throwing themselves off the white cliffs of Dover soon after.

The Reindeer died out in the UK around 8,500 years ago, but in 1952 a Swedish herder brought some over to the Scottish Highlands, where a herd of about 150 lives today.

The Pika

This hamster-like creature is long gone from these shores, but survives in Asia, North America and parts of Eastern Europe, although global warming threatens to propel the cold-preferring pika towards total extinction.

7000 BC

The Tarpan, a type of wild horse from which the common domestic pony is thought to be descended, became extinct in Britain when the land bridge with continental Europe was lost.

6000 BC

The Wolverine

A strong, vicious member of the weasel family, also known as the Glutton: it is even depicted in old Scandinavian documents squeezing itself between trees to help void its stomach. However, its notorious insatiable appetite may be a myth, arising from a mis-translation of its original Swedish name. The word for it in Old Swedish, - *fjellfräs*, meaning "mountain cat" - worked its way into German as *Vielfraß*, which roughly translates as "devours much". It was hunted to extinction in Britain.

1500 BC

The Root Vole had dwelt in Britain when it was still attached to continental Europe, but has been extinct for 5-8000 years.

1000 BC

The Aurochs

A large type of cattle, standing almost a foot taller than modern cows, the aurochs became extinct in Britain during the Bronze Age, and throughout the rest of the world by 1627. Shortly before World War II, geneticist brothers Heinz and Lutz Heck set about recreating the auroch for the Nazis as part of their interest in an idealised 'pure' Teutonic past. They did this by successfully cross-breeding cattle from across Europe which bore a physical resemblance to the ancient beasts. The descendants of these modern aurochs – known as Heck cows - can still be seen near Munich. Indeed a few Heck cows were recently added to a farm in Devon.

500 AD

The Lynx

19th-century experts believed the lynx had been wiped out in Britain by climate change around 3,500 BC, but recent carbon-dating of lynx bones discovered in the 1920s revealed that it was still prowling the isle in 500 AD. Like so many creatures, it was probably extinguished by human hunters.

1000

The Brown Bear

Their enduring popularity with hunters means that only 14,000 brown bears remain in Europe. They have been absent from Britain since the tenth century.

1500

The Wild Boar

It's not known when the last wild boar was hunted down in Britain – perhaps as late as the sixteenth century. James I attempted to reintroduce them to Windsor Great Park in 1610 but was foiled by poachers. In recent decades a handful of boar farms have sprung up in England. The animals have to be kept under strict control, as, even if the farmers and local walkers who value their life think these ferocious hogs are better off in captivity, the boars themselves tend to disagree.

The European Beaver

For centuries the European Beaver was hunted both for its fur and the Castoreum fluid it secretes in its scent glands, sought after as a perfume, a cigarette ingredient, an aphrodisiac, and not least for its purported medical properties such as the cure of epilepsy and the inducement of abortion. As a result the beaver has been extinct in Britain since the sixteenth century, though in recent years a handful have been reintroduced to protected habitats.

1680

The Grey wolf

Britain was the first country to rid itself entirely of the once common wolf, which disappeared from Britain by 1680, its habitat diminished by human occupation. Wolves were also enthusiastically hunted, Edward I having ordered their destruction in 1281. There is currently some talk of reintroducing wolves to the Scottish Highlands.

1700

The Grey Whale

Also known as the Devil Fish and the Rip Sack, the grey whale still exists in the North Pacific, although is in danger of being hunted to extinction – in all likelihood the cause of its demise in British seas in the eighteenth century, too.

c.1840

The Great Bustard

Large, cumbersome and among the heaviest birds capable of flight, you would have thought the Great Bustard would not be an interesting target for hunters – rather like trying to shoot a low-flying sheep. Nevertheless, they were hunted to extinction in the nineteenth century. They have recently been reintroduced on Salisbury plain, and in 2009 three chicks were successfully hatched.

1930

The St. Kilda House Mouse

This large species of house mouse was found only on the islands of the St. Kilda archipelago off Northwest Scotland, possibly brought there by Norse invaders centuries ago. When the St. Kilda inhabitants elected to evacuate to the mainland in 1930, the mouse, an inhabitant exclusively of settlements and houses, was deprived of its habitat and quickly disappeared.

1940

The Kentish Plover

Despite its name, this small bird has shunned Kent – and, indeed, the rest of Britain – in favour of tropical and subtropical climates.

1972

The Burbot

It may look like a typing error, but the freshwater burbot is a relative of the cod. Though common in the North American lakes, there have been no documented catches of this fish in Britain since 1972.

1990

The Greater mouse-eared bat was declared extinct in 1990, but a few individuals have been spotted in Britain in years since, possibly having migrated from Europe. If it does indeed survive, it is the largest British bat.

25

Bon Accord FC:
British Football's Biggest Losers

Bon Accord have entered the record books as the team that received the biggest drubbing in British senior football history. On 12 September 1885, in the first round of the Scottish Cup, they conceded 36 goals to Arbroath, while themselves failing to achieve a single shot on goal for the entire game. Their chances were not helped by the fact that they were actually a cricket team, Orion Cricket Club, who had mistakenly been invited to enter the cup instead of Orion F.C., an Aberdeen football club.

In a remarkable coincidence, just twenty miles away, on the same day and in the same competition, Dundee Harp are recorded as banging in 35 goals against a goal-less Aberdeen Rovers. In fact, the record may rightfully be theirs, since the referee admitted that he had failed to keep accurate count of the number of goals – he reckoned Dundee might in truth have scored 37. However, the Dundee players, in true British sporting fashion, said they had only counted 35 goals, and so this went down as the official score.

'The problem with you, son, is that all your brains are in your head.'

BILL SHANKLY, LIVERPOOL MANAGER, TO A TRAINEE

24

Ethelred the Unready:
What's in a Name?

Ethelred the Unready, or Æthelred Unræd, is a contradiction in terms. His Christian name Ethelred means 'good or noble counsel or advice'; his nickname means 'bad or evil counsel or advice'. He was certainly ill-advised in some of his actions.

Ethelred came to the throne in 978 at the age of ten, after his elder half-brother Edward 'the Martyr' was murdered. From the outset his reign was blighted by the Vikings, who had started raiding Britain and other parts of Europe whenever they had nothing better to do – which was almost all of the time. The raids increased steadily in frequency and in brutality, thrusting deep into the heart of England. Ethelred's army proved useless against them, and he was forced to pay them large bribes, or 'Danegeld', to go away and leave him alone.

As his coffers emptied, Ethelred became desperate, and in 1002 issued one of the most shameful commands ever delivered by an English king. He ordered the massacre of all Danes living in England, to be carried out on St. Bryce's Day – 13 November. The Anglo-Saxons carried out his order with enthusiasm and without mercy, turning ferociously on their Danish neighbours, even though many had lived in England for generations.

The massacre turned out be a very bad political move as well as a moral outrage. Amongst the thousands killed was Gunhilde, sister of Danish King Sweyn Forkbeard.

Sweyn was not the sort to let this kind of thing go unpunished. By 1013, the Danes had overrun the country and Ethelred took to his heels, fleeing to Normandy and ceding the English throne to Sweyn. When Sweyn died a short while later, his son Canute was made king of the northern part of the country, while Ethelred was invited back to be king of the southern part, including London.

Ethelred had inherited an Anglo-Saxon kingdom unified for the first time since the reign of his great-great grandfather, Alfred the Great. By the time he died in 1016, it had become a fief of the Danish Empire.

23

Ronnie Biggs:
Sex, Drugs, Rock 'n' Roll and Robbery

Ronnie Biggs had one very bad decision to thank for his misfortune. In 1963, he accepted an invitation from gang leader Bruce Reynolds to take part in what became known as the most audacious crime in British history – the Great Train Robbery. At the time Biggs was a 34-year-old small-time crook, married with three kids, and going nowhere fast. Along with Reynolds, former boxer Buster Edwards, hairdresser Douglas Goody and London bookie, Charlie Wilson, he stopped the Glasgow to London mail train near Leighton Buzzard on the night of 7 August and, to their collective astonishment, netted a haul of more than £2½ million. Biggs' role in the robbery was to find a train driver who, once the gang had overpowered the real driver, would move the train along the tracks to a suitable spot from where the money could be unloaded into waiting vehicles. For this he was to be paid £40,000.

Such a massive robbery – the biggest ever in Britain – drew a correspondingly massive response from the authorities, and the gang was soon behind bars serving long sentences.

Ronnie Biggs, sentenced to 30 years, had been in prison before and was determined to make this stay a short one. At 3pm on Thursday 8 July, a large furniture-removal van pulled up outside the perimeter wall of Wandsworth prison. While inmates distracted the guards, a couple of rope ladders were tossed over the wall. Biggs and fellow prisoner Eric Flower clambered up, followed by several other opportunistic convicts. They jumped down onto the roof of the van and into a waiting car. After spending time in a safe house they scattered to various locations around the country. Several months after their escape, they were smuggled across the English Channel to Belgium, where they were given new passports and clothes, and underwent painful plastic surgery to change their appearance.

Shortly before Christmas 1965, Biggs travelled to Sydney, Australia, using the alias Terence Furminger. His wife Charmaine and their children joined him and they disappeared into a quiet suburban life until 1969. With the police closing in, however, Biggs decided to flee. He boarded a ship for Panama, flying from there to Brazil, a country that at the time had no extradition agreement with Britain.

Biggs had little of his ill-gotten gains left. Under the alias Michael Haynes, he rented a room in a cheap waterfront hotel, performing odd jobs to eke out an existence. His distance from his family was brought home to him when he learned of the death of his son, Nicky, in a car crash.

He began a relationship with a Brazilian girl, and soon she was pregnant. Biggs, now desperate for money, decided to accept an offer of £50,000 from the *Daily Express* for his story. As he worked on the story with an *Express* journalist, however, the newspaper reduced the offer to £35,000. Biggs had little choice but to accept.

It was all a trick. The *Express* bosses had done a deal with the police to get the story and then have Biggs arrested so that they would not have to hand over any money. On the third day Scotland Yard's Detective Chief Superintendant Jack Slipper – the famous 'Slipper of the Yard', as the tabloids dubbed him – arrived at his door to arrest him.

This time, luck was on Biggs' side. In prison he learned that the Brazilian authorities never deport the father of a Brazilian child, and he walked free, though restricted by a curfew that forced him to remain in Brazil and to be home by ten at night.

Biggs returned to the tabloid front pages in 1978 when Steve Jones and Paul Cook, the remnants of the recently broken-up punk-rock combo the Sex Pistols, arrived in Rio to make a record with him. It was hard to know who was exploiting who, but Biggs never received a penny from the sales of the number 6 hit, *No One Is Innocent*.

In 1981, the unfortunate Biggs was kidnapped by a gang of mercenaries and smuggled onto a yacht that sailed into the Caribbean. The authorities intercepted the vessel off Barbados, and following a court hearing with the world's press looking on, Ronnie was flown back to Rio.

While he had been away, his six-year-old son Michael had appeared on television in a news item about the kidnapping, performing a song and dance routine his father had taught him. It caught the attention of a Brazilian record company that was searching for talented kids to form a group. The Magic Balloon Gang became a pop phenomenon in Brazil, selling 13 million records. Biggs was in the money again. Naturally, he blew it all and before long was again selling his story to anyone who would listen.

Checking his email one day in May 2001, Detective Chief Superintendent John Coles was surprised when an message from Ronnie Biggs popped into his inbox. The 71-year-old Biggs was worn down by his tumultuous life and was unwell. Broke as ever, and having suffered three strokes in two years, he wanted to come home and at last face the music. He told the policeman that he intended to return to Britain to give himself up.

On 7 May, 36 years after he had last set foot on British soil, a private jet brought Ronnie Biggs home. He was met by Coles and a unit of police officers and, back in court that same afternoon, was ordered to serve the remaining 28 years of his original sentence.

His family continued to campaign for his release on compassionate grounds – he had had a fourth stroke, was unable to speak and had to be fed through a tube – but in July 2009 Justice

Secretary Jack Straw refused him parole, claiming that Biggs was 'wholly unrepentant'. But the following month, on the eve of his 80th birthday, he was released, the authorities recognising that by now his health was irreparable.

Before his latest stroke, Biggs had told the BBC: 'My last wish is to walk into a Margate pub as an Englishman and buy a pint of bitter. I hope I live long enough to do that.' Confined again, this time to a hospital bed, it seems unlikely.

EXPRESS DELIVERY, PINT FOR MR BIGGS?

22

Henry VI:
Horrid Henry

Of the eight Henrys whose behinds have warmed the throne of England, the sixth was perhaps the worst. He was pious, indecisive, weak, easily led and frequently insane – and these were among his better qualities. Henry's reign was marked by lawlessness, corruption, treachery and bloodletting almost unmatched in England's history. And for good measure he managed to lose almost all of England's possessions in France, as well as – on two separate occasions – his throne.

On 6 November 1429, a month before his eighth birthday, Henry was crowned King of England at Westminster Abbey. The following month he was crowned King of France at Notre Dame in Paris. So far, so good. But before long the lands that Henry V had gained during the Hundred Years' War began to slip from English control. Joan of Arc led a French military revival and Henry lost his title as King of France.

In 1445 Henry took advantage of peace with France to marry Margaret of Anjou, the niece of the French king. This was no hardship: Margaret was a stunner, and a great deal better at being royal than her husband. There was one snag, however. In return for allowing Henry to marry Margaret, King Charles VII demanded the lands of Maine and Anjou. Henry readily agreed but, aware of the ruckus this would cause in England, neglected to tell anyone. Naturally, when it did come out a year later, there was outrage. By

1450, only Calais remained of England's French possessions, and since the car ferry wouldn't be invented for another few centuries, it was pretty useless.

Meanwhile, England was becoming more and more chaotic. The national coffers were empty, and troops returned unpaid from the war in France. A rebellion led by Jack Cade broke out, and was put down only after much bloodshed.

In 1453, just when it seemed that things could not get any worse, they did. Henry had a mental breakdown. For a year he absented himself from the events of his kingdom, failing to notice even the birth of his son, Edward. The Duke of York was summoned from Ireland and appointed to serve as Protector of the Realm while Henry was ill. On Christmas Day 1454, Henry seemed at last restored to health, but by this time many nobles had had enough of him and put their weight behind York. A violent struggle, the Wars of the Roses, ensued between the houses of York and Lancaster. Henry was deposed by his cousin Edward, who became Edward IV, whereupon he once again descended into madness, allegedly laughing and singing his way through the Battle of St Albans. He and Margaret fled to Scotland, but in 1465 he was captured and imprisoned in the Tower of London.

Queen Margaret formed an alliance with the Earl of Warwick, and with the help of the French king defeated the Yorkists to restore her husband to the throne in 1470. He barely had time to make himself comfortable – enfeebled and unstable, he soon found himself usurped again, and back in the Tower.

On 21 May 1471 this most unpopular and ineffectual of kings was murdered.

21

John Major and 'Back to Basics':
Moral Turpitude in High Places

After the disaster of Black Wednesday on 16 September 1992, when pressure from currency speculators humiliatingly forced Chancellor Norman Lamont to withdraw the pound from the European Exchange Rate Mechanism – a move that cost the country an estimated £3.4 billion – John Major and his government were in sore need of a relaunch. Having failed to protect Britain's economy, they turned their attention to the nation's morality – never a smart thing for a government to do.

At the Tory Party Conference of 1993, Major launched a new crusade, known as 'Back to Basics', and focussing on issues of law and order, education and public probity. Particular emphasis was placed on upholding the sanctity of marriage and reducing the numbers of single mothers at large in the realm.

Unfortunately for Major, several Tory politicians were launching their own private campaigns. Ones which which generally left quite a lot to be desired in the matters of morality and public probity, paid scant attention to the vows of marriage and from time to time actually increased the number of single mothers. For example...

Tim Yeo
The tabloids ruined Minister for the Environment and Countryside Tim Yeo's Christmas holiday when, on Boxing Day

1993, a couple of months after John Major's 'Back to Basics' speech, they revealed that Yeo had added to the 'single mother' stats by fathering a child with Tory councillor Julia Stent. 'YEO HO HO', the headlines sniggered, adding that this was not the first time – he had fathered a child when he was a student, a daughter who was given up for adoption. Yeo resigned.

David Mellor

Chelsea-loving Mellor, Secretary of State for the Department of National Heritage – or 'Minister for Fun' as the tabloid press would have it – was enjoying an affair with the doe-eyed actress Antonia de Sancha in 1992. The *Sun* published a story, which it had received from the renowned publicist Max Clifford, that Mellor had asked de Sancha to let him make love to her wearing a Chelsea strip. There were also stories of a penchant for toe-sucking.

Although he kept his job, his goose was cooked and he was forced to resign a few weeks later after admitting to accepting free holidays from insalubrious people. 'From Toe Job to No Job', mocked the Sun.

Stephen Milligan

When Stephen Milligan, Conservative MP for Eastleigh, was found dead in stockings and suspenders on 7 February 1994, a new sexual practice entered the consciousness of the British public – autoerotic asphyxiation. He had been discovered with a black bin-liner over his head, a satsuma segment in his mouth and an electrical cord tied around his neck in the shape of a noose. John Major, summoning the eloquence for which he was renowned, described his death as 'rather sad'.

Neil Hamilton

In October 1994, the *Guardian* published an article claiming that Corporate Affairs Minister Neil Hamilton and another minister, Tim Smith, had accepted cash from Harrods owner Mohamed Al-Fayed to ask questions in the House of Commons. While Smith did the decent thing – he confessed and resigned – Hamilton hung on until he lost his Parliamentary seat to white-suited former war correspondent Martin Bell in the 1997 general election.

Hamilton was roundly criticised in the report into the Cash for Questions affair and, when he sued Al-Fayed for libel in 1999, was found to have corruptly taken payments from Mobil Oil in 1989. He was declared bankrupt soon after.

Jonathan Aitken

The Chief Secretary to the Treasury and former Minister of State for Defence Procurement resigned to defend himself in 1995, following a *Guardian* investigation into his dealings with prominent Saudis and a Lebanese businessman, and a television programme on the same subject by Granada's *World In Action*.

They alleged that a stay by Aitken at the Ritz in Paris had been paid for by an Arab businessman. Aitken claimed that his wife had paid the hotel bill. When he sued the newspaper and television company for libel, evidence was produced that showed that Mrs Aitken had, in fact, been in Switzerland at the time of the hotel stay. There were also suggestions of shady arms deals.

Aitken had famously claimed at a press conference a few hours before the *World in Action* programme that he would 'cut out the cancer of bent and twisted journalism in our country with the simple sword of truth and the trusty shield of British fair play.' The sword was blunt: the libel case collapsed and he went to prison for perjury and perverting the course of justice.

20

Neil Kinnock:
Pride Comes Before a
Crushing Election Defeat

He should never have said it. It was asking for trouble. A garrotting in *Private Eye* at best; a humiliating snub at the polls by the great British public at worst. But he did say it, and he got both.

On 1 April 1992, having run the gauntlet of 10,000 adoring, high-fiving, backslapping Labour party workers and activists, Neil Kinnock jumped onto the stage and, like a rock star who had been on the road slightly too long or a Southern preacher whose coffers were a little emptier than desired, uttered the fateful words: 'Well, alright!' As if that was not enough, he then uttered them again: 'Well, *alright*!'

And with that double spurt of cringe-making, ill-judged triumphalism, the Labour party's chances of ending fourteen years of Conservative government were summarily scuppered.

Until that hubris-drenched evening at the Sheffield Arena, it had all been going well for Labour. Kinnock had assumed the leadership of the party in 1983, following the train wreck that had been Michael Foot's term in charge. He had modernised the party, and with the help of campaign mastermind Peter Mandelson, ran a credible campaign in the election of 1987, cutting the Tory majority by 42 seats. At the start of April 1992, things were looking hopeful. The Tories seemed to be in decline, the country was sliding into recession, and the memory of the recent poll tax riots lingered like a bad smell around the government of Margaret Thatcher's successor, John Major.

On the morning of 1 April – 'Red Wednesday', as it was dubbed – the opinion polls showed Labour with a clear lead. Next morning, after the Labour leadership had been vaingloriously introduced at the Sheffield Arena as 'the next foreign secretary', 'the next Home Secretary', 'the next Prime Minister', and so on, the lead had vanished. Some polls even showed the Conservatives ahead.

A week later, on election day, Neil Kinnock picked up the morning papers to be greeted by the *Sun*'s famous headline: **'IF KINNOCK WINS TODAY WILL THE LAST PERSON TO LEAVE BRITAIN PLEASE TURN OUT THE LIGHTS'.** He knew at once it was all over.

The Conservatives were returned to Government with a reduced majority of 21 seats, and Neil Kinnock turned out to be merely the John the Baptist to Tony Blair's Jesus. He disappeared into the wilderness of the European Commission.

'The Labour Party's election manifesto is the longest suicide note in history.'

GERALD KAUFMAN, LABOUR PARTY POLITICIAN ABOUT HIS OWN PARTY'S LEFT-WING 1983 ELECTION MANIFESTO

BRITISH ELECTORAL LOSERS SINCE 1800: THE LEADERS OF THE TWO MAIN PARTIES WHO NEVER WON GENERAL ELECTIONS

Year	Party	Leader
1802	Whigs	Charles James Fox
1812	Whigs	George Ponsonby
1818	Whigs	George Tierney
1826 & 1830	Whigs	Marquess of Lansdowne
1841	Whigs	William Lamb
1906	Labour	Keir Hardie
1918	Labour	William Adamson
1922	Labour	John Robert Clynes
1931	Labour	Arthur Henderson
1959	Labour	Hugh Gaitskell
1983	Labour	Michael Foot
1987 & 1992	Labour	Neil Kinnock
2001	Conservatives	William Hague
2005	Conservatives	Michael Howard

A special mention goes to Iain Duncan Smith, Conservative Leader of the Opposition, 2001-3, who failed even to make it to a general election before being booted out by his party.

19

Captain Lawrence 'Titus' Oates:
'I Am Just Going Outside…'

Lawrence Edward Grace Oates puts the 'Great' into 'Great British Loser'. He provides a matchless example of the stiff upper lip in the face of dire adversity.

Oates was educated at Eton, before becoming a professional soldier in the 6th Iniskilling Dragoons, an elite cavalry regiment. He was recommended for the Victoria Cross for his bravery in the Boer War, during which he received a bullet wound to the thigh that left him with a pronounced limp and a left leg two inches shorter than the right.

After the war, however, Oates became disenchanted with the army. His chance to leave came in 1909, when he heard of Captain Robert Falcon Scott's plans to travel to the South Pole. Despite his leg injury and lack of any qualifications whatever for the task of dragging a sledge nearly 1,800 miles across the most inhospitable landscape in the world, Oates was accepted onto the expedition – largely, perhaps, because of his personal donation of £1,000 (roughly equivalent to £50,000 today). On 1 November 1911, Scott, Oates and fourteen others set off from their base camp at Cape Evans.

The only cavalryman amongst a team of sailors, Oates made himself useful by looking after the nineteen ponies during the first half of the 895-mile trek to the Pole, and preparing food depots for their return journey. But his diaries show him lonely and glum,

186

and annoyed by Scott's poor leadership and moodiness. At one point he wrote, 'Myself, I dislike Scott intensely and would chuck the whole thing if it were not that we are a British expedition... He is not straight, it is himself first, the rest nowhere.' They clashed over the organisation of supplies for the return leg, the squeamish Scott rejecting Oates' suggestion of taking the ponies as near to the Pole as possible, then shooting them for food. Furthermore, Scott refused to build the vital last depot thirty miles nearer the Pole, as Oates had advised. The following year these decisions were to prove critical, as the freezing, starving men battled their way back from the Pole through pitiless weather.

His misery and physical limitations notwithstanding, Oates was included in the five-man party to travel the final 167 miles to the Pole, which they reached on 17 January 1912, seventy-nine days after departing base camp.

Unfortunately, it was only to discover that the Norwegian explorer Roald Amundsen had beaten them to it by five weeks.

On their desperate return journey, dejected by the failure of their venture, Scott's flagging team was hampered by frostbite, food shortages and the unusually harsh Antarctic summer, which that year was ten degrees colder than average. Compounding their difficulties was the fact that Scott had weighed down their sledges with an extra thirty kilos of geological samples. On 17 February, Scott's long-time team-mate Edgar Evans died, weakened by a head injury he had sustained falling down a crevasse a few days before. The other four struggled on, but Oates was by now severely debilitated by frostbite and gangrene in his feet, and was also suffering from scurvy, which had caused his old leg wound to become a suppurating mess. His pace slowed until he was only able to walk three miles a day, a third of the daily distance they needed to cover.

On 15 March Oates implored the team to continue without him. They refused, of course, but Oates knew that their only chance of survival hinged on his own self-sacrifice. On the morning of 16 March 1912, the day before his 32nd birthday, Lawrence Oates uttered his famous parting shot: 'I am just going outside and may be some time.' Not bothering to put on his boots, he crawled from the tent into a blizzard and a temperature of -40°C, and died very near the spot where he had proposed positioning the depot.

Sadly this act did not save the rest of the team. On 29 March they died in their tent, a mere eleven miles from the depot.

'Myself, I dislike Scott intensely and would chuck the whole thing if it were not that we are a British expedition... He is not straight, it is himself first, the rest nowhere.'

CAPTAIN LAWRENCE 'TITUS' OATES

18

Nick Leeson:
What's a Few Hundred Million
Between Friends?

A t 5:46 am on 17 January 1995, an earthquake measuring
7.3 on the Richter Scale devastated the Japanese city of
Kobe, killing around 4,600 people and making almost quarter of
a million homeless. It also precipitated the downfall of Britain's
oldest merchant bank, the 233-year-old Barings.

As he woke to the news of the earthquake, Nick Leeson, general
manager of Barings' Singapore futures markets operation, might
well have wished that he was standing at its epicentre. He had
just placed a gargantuan bet that the Nikkei Index would not
drop below 19,000 points. But the earthquake had sent the Asian
markets into free-fall, and they continued to plummet for the rest
of that week.

In this particular case Leeson may have been the victim of misfortune, but the wager was by no means the first bad decision he
had made in his time in Singapore.

Born on a Watford council estate, Leeson did not distinguish
himself at school, failing maths and leaving with few qualifications. Nevertheless, in the early 1980s he managed to get a job
with Coutts, the royal bank. He later worked for a number of other
banks before arriving at Barings, where he impressed his employ-
ers sufficiently to be offered a position on the trading floor.

Leeson was soon sent to Singapore, where his job was to bet on the future direction of the Nikkei Index. To start with he seemed to be doing well. In 1993, his first year, he made Barings £10 million – 10% of their entire year's profit. And of course Leeson himself profited too, with a bonus of £150,000 to add to his £50,000 annual salary. He and his wife Lisa lived the good life.

Behind the scenes, however, all was not well. Barings' bosses had failed to spot that Leeson was actually using their own money, rather than that of their clients, to make his bets. A fund had previously been established to cover a mistake by another Barings employee, and as Leeson's losses mounted, he began to use this account, named 88888 – the number 8 ironically representing good luck in Chinese numerology – to cover his own losses. By Christmas 1994, his losses in account 88888 totalled a staggering £208 million.

Leeson became progressively unhinged, and was arrested for an incident when he showed his backside to two women. The Barings executives ordered a cover-up, and remained supportive.

Then the earthquake hit Kobe.

Leeson continued desperately to make deals, counting on a post-quake bounce that never materialised. Barings even allocated him fresh funds to continue trading – until, that is, his horrified bosses discovered the full extent of the catastrophe he had engineered. With losses amounting to £827 million, twice the bank's available trading capital, Barings went bust on 26 February 1994, with 1,200 people losing their jobs. The Dutch bank ING bought the centuries-old company for £1, assuming all of its debt.

By this time the rogue trader was already gone, his wife in tow, having left a scribbled note on his desk saying, 'I'm sorry.'

The couple fled to Malaysia, then on to Thailand and then Germany. Leeson knew he faced imprisonment for what he had done, but hoped that by coming to Europe he might be jailed in Britain rather than in one of Singapore's primitive prisons. His efforts were to no avail, and on 2 March he was sent back to face fraud charges.

He was sentenced to six and a half years in prison, during which he 'found God', was divorced by Lisa and was diagnosed with colon cancer.

Nick Leeson lost bigger than most. Spare your tear ducts, though. He beat the cancer and moved to Ireland, where for a time he was Chief Executive of football team Galway United. When he wasn't regaling audiences on the after-dinner circuit, that is.

He still dabbles in the stock market, but these days he uses his own money.

In December 1938, Lloyds of London was offering odds of 32 to 1 that there would be no war in the following year.

In 1939, World War II began.

17

Admiral Byng:
Pour Encourager Les Autres

John Byng's father was an eminent admiral who had been created 1st Viscount Torrington as a reward for his stalwart service to the country. When his son enlisted in the Royal Navy at the age of 14, it seemed certain he would follow in his father's footsteps, and before long Byng Jr. was indeed rising through the ranks. He became a lieutenant at 19, and four years later was Captain of HMS *Gibraltar* as it patrolled (uneventfully, for the most part) in the Mediterranean.

In 1745 he was made rear admiral, and in 1747 a vice-admiral. However, his postings were invariably quiet, and by 1756, when he was serving in the Channel, he had yet to see enemy action.

That all changed very fast when Byng, now a full Admiral, was given orders to relieve the British garrison at Fort St. Philip on the island of Minorca, where a French naval attack had long been expected. From the start Byng felt that he had not been given adequate funds, time, equipment or men to fulfill the operation properly. As his enraged letters to the Admiralty show, he set sail convinced that his mission was doomed to failure.

He arrived off Minorca on 19 May, and the following day was attacked by 15,000 French troops. The encounter did not go well. Byng missed several opportunities to assail the superior French squadron, which, having severely damaged the British fleet, got away unscathed. After four days' ineffectual loitering just off

Minorca, too weak either to relieve the beleaguered fort or to make a second assault on the French fleet, Byng and his Council of War decided to head for the port of Gibraltar to have their wounded men treated and their ships repaired. Before they reached port, however, a British ship intercepted them. Byng was relieved of his command and arrested.

Minorca fell to the French on 29 June, provoking popular outrage in Britain, where Byng's failure to relieve the garrison or pursue the French was seen as little short of cowardice. The Admiral was brought back to Portsmouth, where he was court-martialed under the Articles of War, which had been recently amended to mandate capital punishment for any officer who 'failed to do his utmost' against the enemy. Despite numerous pleas for clemency by those who felt Byng was being made a scapegoat for the Government and the Admiralty's failure to act quickly enough, King George II chose not to exercise his Royal Pardon. When Prime Minister Pitt told him that the House of Commons was inclined to mercy, His Germanic Majesty tersely replied to the effect that Pitt had taught him not to expect common sense from the House of Commons.

On 14 March 1757 Admiral John Byng was executed, the last British Admiral to suffer this fate. His descendants are still seeking a posthumous pardon.

'In England, it is thought wise to kill an admiral from time to time, to encourage the others.'

VOLTAIRE

16

Captain Edward John Smith:
That Sinking Feeling

By April 1912, Captain Edward Smith had risen to the very summit of his profession. He was one of the world's most experienced captains, and the highest echelons of English society demanded that he command the ships on which they sailed. Not for nothing was he known as the 'Millionaires' Captain'.

After an unimpeachable apprenticeship as a merchant seaman, Smith had joined the White Star Line in 1880 and went on to captain no fewer than seventeen of the line's ships, rising through the ranks to Commander and acquiring a reputation as a 'safe' captain. However as the vessels he commanded got bigger and more unwieldy, this claim began to be put to the test. In February 1899 the *Germanic*, under his command, capsized at her moorings due to the build-up of ice on her rigging and superstructure.

In 1911 he was given command of the *Olympic*, at the time the largest ship in the world, on its maiden voyage from Liverpool to New York. The ship negotiated the mid Atlantic currents successfully, but as she was docking in New York harbour on 21 June, one of the twelve tugs assisting the manoeuvre got caught in her backwash. The tug was briefly trapped beneath the liner, only just managing to free itself before either vessel was significantly damaged.

Later that year, the *Olympic* collided with the British warship HMS *Hawke*. The warship lost its prow, while the *Olympic*'s propeller was twisted and two of her watertight compartments flooded. The *Olympic*, with Smith at the helm, was blamed for the incident and The White Star Line was hamstrung financially while the liner was out of service. To make matters worse, the completion of the company's new liner, RMS *Titanic*, was delayed while repairs were carried out on *Olympic*.

Despite these warning signs, the illustrious Smith was given command of the *Titanic* for its maiden voyage from Southampton to New York in April 1912. It was rumoured that it would be Smith's last voyage before retirement – he was 62 years old – but other reports suggested that he would be taking command of another, even bigger ship, the *Gigantic*, once she was completed.

At midday on 10 April, as *Titanic* left Southampton Docks, the huge swell she created caused the berthed SS *New York* to break free from her moorings and almost collide with her. Smith avoided catastrophe by taking swift evasive action. Nonetheless, the incident caused unease.

Titanic called at the French port of Cherbourg, then at Cobh in Ireland, picking up extra passengers before heading off into the Atlantic. At twenty minutes to midnight on the night of 14 April, she struck an iceberg. Three hours later she sank, breaking in two as she did so. Over 1500 people lost their lives, including Captain Smith.

He is said to have been uncharacteristically indecisive during the crisis, first ordering that the lifeboats be prepared, then hesitating when it was time for them to be lowered. The crew did not carry out several of his commands because believed them to be unsound. His last confirmed action was to give the order to abandon ship.

There are conflicting versions of his death. One passenger claimed to have seen him raise a pistol to his head and shoot himself on the bridge. Another reported seeing him swimming towards a raft with a baby in his arms, while others testified that he walked calmly onto the bridge and went down with his ship.

'The captain may, by simply moving an electric switch, instantly close the watertight doors throughout, making the vessel virtually unsinkable.'

THE SHIPBUILDER AND MARINE ENGINE BUILDER
DESCRIBING TITANIC IN JUNE 1911

15

Field Marshall John French, 1st Earl of Ypres: Catastrophic Commander

French was the disastrous Commander-in-Chief of the British Expeditionary Force (BEF) at the start of the First World War. From the outset his fiery temper and argumentative nature got him into hot water, as he argued with Field Marshal Lord Kitchener and General Sir Douglas Haig about the most effective deployment of his troops. He said Belgium; they said Amiens. They were right.

French was guilty both of procrastination and of hasty decisions, as when he ordered his troops to abandon positions during the first battles at Mons and Le Cateau. Fortunately, on this occasion General Sir Horace Smith-Dorrien ignored his orders and mounted a defensive action that allowed the troops to make an orderly withdrawal.

As his relationship with Kitchener deteriorated, French oversaw the defeat of the last of the BEF at Neuve Chapelle and Ypres. He then refused to cooperate with the French in 1915 and was finally relieved of his command, to be replaced by Sir Douglas Haig (see overleaf).

Naturally, he was rewarded for his efforts with a peerage and command of the army in Ireland. He went on to oversee the brutal suppression of the 1916 Easter Rising.

14

Field Marshall Sir Douglas Haig: The Butcher of the Somme

Douglas Haig was a cavalry man through and through. The First World War, with soldiers bogged down in stalemated trench warfare was completely alien to him. 'The machine gun is a much over rated weapon,' he said in 1915. He was similarly contemptuous about the tank.

Haig's name will forever be associated with the Somme offensive that began on 1 July 1916. The purpose of the action was to relieve the French forces at Verdun.

The infamous first day of the Somme attack saw staggering casualty figures – 60,000, by far the largest in British military history – and the slaughter continued for four and a half months until 18 November 1916, when Haig called it off. Technically it had been a British victory, but there was minimal strategic gain.

Another mighty battle was fought at Passchendaele in 1917, again at horrific cost to the British army.

Towards the end of the war, Haig began to advocate a compromise peace to bring the conflict to a conclusion. He claimed that the French army was exhausted and the Americans were in a state of disarray, and worried that the Bolsheviks would overrun Germany if the peace terms were too harsh. Basically he wanted to leave Germany armed and with its territorial gains intact.

Arguments have raged about Haig in recent decades. He is perhaps the most criticized leader in British military history, portrayed either as a butcher who sent millions of men to their death or as an incompetent bungler, or both.

Yet to many of his contemporaries Haig was a hero, and at his state funeral in 1928 crowds lined the streets of London. In fact, more people showed up to it than to the funeral of Princess Diana. It was after he was dead that his reputation began to lose its sheen. Churchill accused him of blocking enemy machine gun fire with 'the breasts of good men.' For Lloyd George, in his *War Memoirs*, Haig was 'intellectually and temperamentally unequal to his task'. Lloyd George claimed that Haig surrounded himself with 'gentlemen' in preference to good military advisers, and that he did not understand the complexities of the Western Front.

Historian Paul Fusell condemned him as 'stubborn, self-righteous, inflexible, intolerant – especially of the French – and quite humourless... Indeed, one powerful legacy of Haig's performance is the conviction among the imaginative and intelligent today of the unredeemable defectiveness of all civil and military leaders. Haig could be said to have established the paradigm.'

Haig was brutally satirized in the performance of John Mills in the musical film *Oh What a Lovely War!*, but perhaps the most cutting remark about him came in *Blackadder Goes Forth*, when the eponymous hero says: 'Haig is about to make yet another gargantuan effort to move his drinks cabinet six inches closer to Berlin.'

'The idea that cavalry will be replaced by these iron coaches is absurd. It is little short of treasonous.'

COMMENT OF AN AIDE-DE-CAMP TO FIELD MARSHAL HAIG,
AT A TANK DEMONSTRATION, 1916.

13

Neville Chamberlain:
'Peace For Our Time...'

Neville Chamberlain, British Prime Minister from May 1937 until May 1940, achieved many things. He secured the passage of the Factories Act of 1937, which obtained better working conditions in factories and limited the hours worked by women and children. He was also responsible for the Holidays with Pay Act, which recommended (you guessed it) paid holidays.

Yet it is not as a domestic reformer that Chamberlain has gone down in the annals of history. Instead, his name will forever conjure an image of a thin, dark-coated man, triumphantly clutching a piece of paper that he claimed would bring 'Peace for our time'. His high spirits would have been somewhat dampened had he known that at around the same time in Germany, Adolf Hitler's Foreign Minister Joachim von Ribbentrop was remonstrating with the Führer for signing the agreement. Hitler's reply? 'Oh, don't take it so seriously. That piece of paper is of no further significance whatever.'

And so it turned out a year later, when Hitler sent his troops into Poland. Chamberlain duly declared war, and remained in office for eight months before resigning in favour of Winston Churchill.

Although he served in the war cabinet, Chamberlain was deeply depressed by his failure to prevent war and by the manner in which his premiership had ended. 'Few men,' he wrote, 'can have known such a reversal of fortune in so short a time.'

12

Pete Best:
The Beatle Who Never Was

Did Pete Best lose out on a life of fortune and fame merely because his hair was too curly?

In late 1961 John Lennon was given £100 by an aunt for his 21st birthday. He and Paul McCartney decided to spend the money on a holiday in Paris, where they visited Jürgen Vollmer, a German friend they'd met in Hamburg. The two Beatles had always liked the way Vollmer wore his hair. It was flattened down with a fringe at the front – a very different style to the Brylcreemed, 'duck's ass' they sported at the time. They asked Vollmer to cut their hair in the same style, and the Beatles' 'moptop' was born. Back in Liverpool, they encouraged the other band members to adopt the same style. However, as their friend the German photographer Astrid Kirchherr has pointed out: 'Pete has really curly hair, and it wouldn't work.'

Best's refusal to change his hairstyle, or the impossibility of so doing, are just two of the explanations cited for Best's dismissal as drummer of The Beatles on 16 August 1962. The reason the other Beatles gave him was that he was just not a good enough drummer, and that George Martin wouldn't offer the band a contract if he remained. Yet another rumour has it that he was sacked after rejecting the advances of Brian Epstein, the band's gay manager. It has also been suggested that the other members of the group – especially Paul McCartney – were jealous of the attention he was receiving from adoring female fans.

It may well have been a case of Best simply not fitting in. Lennon, Harrison and McCartney hung out together, but Best always remained aloof, avoiding the drug culture to which the others had been introduced in Hamburg and refusing to take Preludin stimulants to stay awake during their long shows. And on stage he looked different to the others (hairstyle apart), wearing a white shirt while they slouched in leather jackets, jeans and cowboy boots.

Best was sacked almost two years after he had joined the group, and just two months before The Beatles recorded their first single, 'Love Me Do'. John Lennon, for one, was not proud of the mode of his dismissal. 'We were cowards,' he said later. 'We got Epstein to do the dirty work for us.' Ringo Starr, who had stood in for Best when he was ill, joined the band, and within six months The Beatles had become a pop phenomenon.

Pete Best drew the curtains, locked the doors and stayed home for two weeks after his dismissal. He then emerged to make a couple of unsuccessful stabs at fame with other bands in Britain and America. At one point he contemplated suicide, but was talked out of it by his mother and his brother. Eventually, he packed in showbiz altogether, taking a job loading bread onto delivery vans and marrying a woman called Kathy who worked on the biscuit counter at Woolworth's. After that, he became a civil servant for twenty years, attaining a smidgeon of celebrity as the man The Beatles left behind.

In a financial sense at least, his story does have a happy ending. When the three surviving Beatles and John Lennon's widow, Yoko Ono, released the *Anthology* albums, they included ten early Beatles songs on which Pete Best drummed. The album on which he played became one of the bestselling of all time, and Best is reputed to have earned £4 million in royalties.

THE OTHERS WHO MISSED OUT ON BEATLEMANIA

Pete Best wasn't the only one to miss out on the riches and adulation enjoyed by the Fab Four. Another 15 guitarists, drummers, washboard and tea chest players could have enjoyed Beatlemania if they had not got sick, gone to uni, had to do their National Service, argued on the bus, etc, etc.

Pete Shotton

Shotton grew up with John Lennon, attending the same schools and playing the washboard in the future Beatle's first band, skiffle outfit The Quarrymen. Fired around the time Paul McCartney joined, Lennon marked his friend's departure in characteristic style – he smashed a washboard over Shotton's head at a party. When The Beatles first tasted success, Lennon bought his old friend a supermarket on Hayling Island. Shotton then managed the Beatles' doomed retail venture, the Apple Boutique. before becoming managing director of their company Apple Corps. When Apple began to rot, Shotton returned to his supermarket on Hayling Island. In the late 1970s he launched the initially successful Fatty Arbuckle's restaurant chain, which he sold before retiring in comfortable tax exile in Dublin.

Eric Griffiths

Taught the banjo by Lennon's mother, Griffiths was a founder member of The Quarrymen. When Harrison joined the band, he was asked to buy an electric bass and an amplifier, but he couldn't afford them, and was not invited to the next rehearsal. He enlisted in the Merchant Navy, before joining the Prison Service and then operating a chain of dry cleaners. He died, aged 64, in 2005.

Colin Hanton

Apprentice upholsterer Hanton was asked to join The Quarrymen mainly because he owned a drum kit. He left the band after an argument on the bus home about a catastrophic gig they had just played at the Pavilion Theatre in 1959. His drumming can be heard on *In Spite of All the Danger* and *That'll be the Day* on The Beatles' album *Anthology 1*. He still works in the upholstery business.

Rod Davis

Davis, who first met Lennon at Sunday School and played football with him as a small boy, was asked to join The Quarrymen in 1956 after buying a banjo. He left the band before Paul McCartney joined in 1957, and has worked in a variety of jobs. He still plays guitar in a number of folk and bluegrass bands.

Ivan Vaughan

A boyhood friend of Lennon, Ivan Vaughan was the bass player in The Quarrymen and was famously responsible for introducing him to Paul McCartney at the Woolton Village Fete on 6 July 1957. He left the band to become a teacher, but was on the books of Apple for a spell, given the task of establishing a school that embodied the alternative values of the Sixties. In 1977, he was diagnosed with Parkinson's Disease about which he wrote a book that was published in 1986. He also featured in a Jonathan Miller BBC documentary about his search for a cure. After his death in

1993, Paul McCartney wrote a poem about him, *Ivan*, that was included in his book of poems, *Blackbird Singing*.

Bill Smith

Smith plucked the string of a tea chest with the Quarrymen at a few early gigs.

Nigel Whalley

Another early Quarrymen tea chest player, Whalley, working at the time as an apprentice golf professional, was their acting manager until he contracted tuberculosis in 1958.

Len Garry

Yet another tea chest player who was in The Quarrymen until August 1958 when he became seriously ill with meningitis. He later became an architect.

John Duff Lowe

Lowe joined the band in 1958 but left soon after because the journey from his home to rehearsals at Paul McCartney's house was too far. He also had a girlfriend who grumbled about him not spending time with her. Instead of becoming a moptop, he became a stockbroker and banker.

Ken Brown

Brown played in The Quarrymen with Lennon and McCartney for a while, but was thrown out of the band after an argument about money. He played in the Blackjacks with Pete Best until Best joined The Beatles just before their first trip to Hamburg. He died aged 70 in 2010.

Arthur Kelly

Bass player Kelly was invited to join the band before they went to Hamburg but he turned them down. He went on to become an actor, appearing in *Coronation Street* and countless other TV dramas.

Stuart Sutcliffe

Sutcliffe was the original Silver Beetles bass player, joining the band in 1959. Having fallen in love with photographer Astrid Kirchherr, he stayed in Germany when the band returned to Liverpool, enrolling at the Hamburg College of Art. He died suddenly of a brain haemorrhage in April 1962, just months before The Beatles recorded their first single, *Love Me Do*.

Tommy Moore

Moore drummed for The Silver Beatles on the 1960 'Beat Ballad' tour of northeast Scotland, during which they backed teen heartthrob Johnny Gentle. He died in 1981.

Norman Chapman

After Moore left the band, Chapman became their drummer during July and August 1960. He left to do his National Service.

Chas Newby

Newby played four gigs, including the famous one at the Litherland Town Hall on 27 December 1960, when 'Beatlemania' is said to have been born. He turned down an invitation to become the band's permanent bass player to go to university. He later became a maths teacher.

11

Jimmy 'The Whirlwind' White: Pot Lack

Jimmy White's best teacher was a character called Dodgy Bob, who taught him how to hustle. He first came across Bob at the age of eleven, when he was supposed to be attending Ernest Bevin Comprehensive in his native Tooting. He and his friend, Tony Meo – no mean snooker player himself in later life – spent every spare minute hitting balls around the green baize at Zan's Hall Billiard Club. By thirteen White had made his first century break – he has made 287 in his career – and had begun to put Dodgy Bob's tutelage to good use, hustling money from Zan's regulars. It was at this time that he acquired the nickname 'The Whirlwind', due to the audacious pace at which he played the game.

Jimmy soon graduated from the murky penumbra of Zan's to the bright lights of television, and rapidly became a favourite with the viewing audience. This was snooker's golden age – Steve Davis, Alex Higgins, John Parrot and Dennis Taylor were all potting balls at the time – but it was White who thrilled the punters most.

Meanwhile he enjoyed the good life outside the world of snooker. In 1994, after winning £128,000 for his first World Championship maximum break, he blew the lot on cards and horses. He once disappeared for five whole weeks, and marathon binges were common occurrences. Unsurprisingly, such behaviour affected not only his game but also his family life. His marriage came under strain.

White's first experience of the Embassy World Championship Final came in 1984. He trailed his opponent, Steve Davis, by 12-4 at the end of the first day's play, and a typically gutsy comeback was not quite enough. He lost 18-16.

Six years later he was back again, but was outplayed by his nemesis Stephen Hendry, who beat White in the final for the first of four times. In 1991 John Parrot slaughtered him 18-11, but in 1992 White led Hendry 12-6, then 14-8. He came within a single red of winning the 24th and 25th frames but missed them both. He continued to falter, and in the end Hendry took the title 18-14 after an amazing ten-frame winning streak,

In the final of 1993, White's game was no match for Hendry at the height of his powers. The Whirlwind was destroyed by 18 frames to 5.

Remarkably, White reached his fifth consecutive World Final in 1994, when he again faced Hendry. He quickly fell behind by 5 frames to 1, but staged a tenacious fightback to lead 10-9. In the 34th frame, White took the match to a final frame with a courageous break of 75. He led the decisive frame by 37 points to 24, but as had happened so often, he blew it, missing an easy black. Hendry cleared the table to win the fourth of his seven World Championships.

Jimmy White won ten major ranking tournaments and picked up around £5 million in prize money, but he will forever be remembered for what he didn't do – win the World title.

'I think it's great to talk during sex, as long as it's about snooker.'

STEVE DAVIS

MORE BRITISH SPORTSMEN WHO FAILED TO WIN THE BIG ONE

Steve Backley
Javelin-thrower Backley won four European gold medals and three Commonwealths, but when it came to World Championships and the Olympics he never did better than silver.

Sir Henry Cooper
Despite a glittering career in which he became the only British boxer to win three Lonsdale Belts outright and the first person to put Muhammad Ali – then fighting as Cassius Clay – on the canvas, the oft-cut Cooper never even fought for the World Championship, turning down fights with champions Floyd Paterson and Sonny Liston. Rejecting a fight with Liston, his manager Jim Wicks famously said, 'We don't even want to meet Liston walking down the same street.'

Herol 'Bomber' Graham
Acknowledged as one of the best British boxers never to win a world title, southpaw Graham fought for it three times at middleweight and super-middleweight, but lost on each occasion.

Colin Jackson
He held world record for the 110 metres that remained unbro-

ken for a remarkable ten years, won two Commonwealth Games gold medals, three World Championship gold medals and enjoyed a 12-year winning streak in the European Championships. The Olympics? A silver in 1992 in Barcelona, but Jackson never stood grinning on the top step of the Olympic podium.

Colin Montgomerie

Montgomerie has gurned his way to second place in five majors, most notably losing in a three-way play-off to Ernie Els in the US Open in 1994. The next year, he lost in a play-off for the US PGA Championship. Two years later, despite recording one of the greatest rounds in US Open history – a 65 – he lost by one stroke, again to Els. In 2005, he finished second to Tiger Woods in the US Open and in 2006 led the same tournament on the 18th, but blew it, to lose by one shot. In autumn 2010, Montgomerie captained the European team to victory in the Ryder Cup. Some consolation, perhaps…

Sir Stirling Moss

Second four times in a row, Stirling Moss is universally recognized as the best driver never to win the Formula One World Championship.

Paula Radcliffe

She nods her way to victory in marathons all over the world and has held more athletics world records than you can shake a stick at. But she is above all remembered for her emotional implosion at the Athens Olympics. She has one last shot in 2012, but at the time of writing has still to wear Olympic gold round her neck.

10

King John:
A Right Royal Loser

Poor John, younger brother to crusading hero King Richard the Lionheart, had a lot to live up to – and he didn't come close. He lost his French possessions (hence his traditional nickname 'Lackland'), and almost lost his English ones in a civil war (his other nickname was 'Softsword'). He also succeeded in getting the country excommunicated by the Pope, was forced by his barons to sign the humiliating Magna Carta, and went down in history as the nasty in the Robin Hood legend. To cap it all, he lost the crown jewels in the Wash.

He died shortly after this last fiasco, probably of embarrassment, though his death is attributed by some chroniclers to a surfeit of unripe fruit.

9

Bill Boaks:
Serial Electoral Deposit Loser

They just don't make them any more like Lieutenant Commander William George Boaks, campaigner for road safety, deposit-loser in countless elections, and longstanding holder of the record for the lowest number of votes in a British by-election – five, in the 1982 Glasgow Hillhead by-election.

Bill Boaks, who had enjoyed a distinguished naval career, launched the first of his many campaigns to get elected to Parliament in 1951, when he stood in the Walthamstow East constituency, representing his 'Admiral party' (Association of Democratic Monarchists Representing All Women). His plan had been to drum up publicity by standing against the Prime Minister, Clement Atlee, but he made one critical error: he had put himself forward as a candidate for Walthamstow East, whereas Atlee's constituency was Walthamstow *West*. Boaks received 174 votes.

He went on to stand in more than 40 elections, invariably losing his deposit. Most often he campaigned on a platform of road safety, on which subject he had some novel ideas. For instance, he argued that, instead of Zebra crossings marking the only places where roads could safely be crossed, the entire road should be treated as if it were a Zebra crossing, with small areas painted to indicate where crossing was *not* permitted. He would regularly push a pram filled with bricks very slowly across Zebra crossings, and once even went so far as to sit in a deckchair in the middle of the very busy Westway dual carriageway, where he calmly perused the *Daily Telegraph*.

It is a sad irony that this tireless, eccentric campaigner for better road safety ended his life due to a road accident. He was injured as he stepped off a bus, and died two years later, on 4 April 1986, as a result of head injuries he had sustained during the accident.

8

Percy Pilcher:
So Near and Yet So Far

So often there is no more than a hair's breadth between eternal fame and pitiable obscurity, for cruel history remembers only the winner. With this in mind, Percy Sinclair Pilcher may be one of the greatest losers of them all.

A keen inventor, Pilcher had a passion for aviation, and spent much of his time building gliders. His first hang-glider, *The Bat*, made its inaugural flight in 1895 on a hill by the Forth of Clyde. Later that year, Pilcher went to Berlin to meet Otto Lilienthal, Germany's leading glider expert. With Lilienthal's advice, Pilcher built two more gliders, *The Beetle* and *The Gull*, but in August 1896 his mentor was killed when his glider stalled in mid flight in Berlin. Pilcher went on to build his fourth glider, *The Hawk*. In it he achieved a world distance record in 1897, when he flew 820 feet in the grounds of Stanford Hall, a country house in Leicestershire.

Meanwhile, powered flight was emerging as Pilcher's new obsession. He considered adding an engine to *The Hawk,* but couldn't find one light enough for the structure. He invented a triplane, with a four-horsepower petrol engine and two propellers, but he ran out of money before the machine could be completed. To raise the necessary funds, Pilcher arranged a demonstration of his 'soaring machine' at Stanford Hall on 30 September 1899.

On both sides of the Atlantic the race to achieve powered flight had been followed avidly, and the audience of potential sponsors was agog to see his demonstration. Pilcher, too, was feverish with anticipation: just a little more cash and a few more days, and he would be in a position to make his engine work properly, and write the Pilcher name into the history books. Unfortunately, however, the triplane's engine was malfunctioning that day, and the weather was also too stormy to attempt the flight. Rather than disappoint the crowd, Pilcher took the fateful decision to strap himself into his glider, *The Hawk*.

As he soared to a height of thirty feet the audience gazed skywards in awe, but gasped in horror as the tail snapped off the craft, sending *The Hawk* plummeting to the ground. Pilcher was dragged from the wreckage unconscious and rushed to hospital, where he died two days later, aged just thirty-two.

Four years later, on 17 December 1903, the Wright Brothers flew into history when they performed the first powered flight at an airfield in Kitty Hawk, North Carolina.

Would Percy Pilcher have done it? In 2003, the School of Aeronautics at Cranfield University was commissioned by BBC's *Horizon* to build a workable replica of his triplane. It achieved a sustained, controlled flight for one minute and 25 seconds – 26 seconds longer than the Wright brothers managed on the day they became immortal.

'There is an art… to flying. The knack lies in learning how to throw yourself at the ground and miss.'

DOUGLAS ADAMS, *THE HITCHHIKERS GUIDE TO THE GALAXY*

7

Beagle 2: Mars 3

Fans of the euphemism all over the country went wild with delight when scientists announced that Beagle 2 had made a 'hard landing' on the surface of Mars.

In other words, it had crashed.

The £44-million venture was conceived by a group of British scientists led by the mutton-chop-whiskered Professor Colin Pillinger of the Open University – the man who, in spite of the utter failure of his pet project, would become Britain's favourite scientist.

Named after Charles Darwin's ship, the spacecraft's mission was to search for signs of life on Mars. It was launched from Baikonur in Kazakhstan on 2 June 2003, and separated from its mount, the *Mars Express Orbiter,* on 19 December.

It was never heard from again.

'I am strongly opposed to Charles going on this Beagle *voyage. He is moving away from the Church, drifting irretrievably into a life of sport and idleness.'*

ROBERT WARING DARWIN, CHARLES DARWIN'S FATHER

6

Sir Clive Sinclair and the Sinclair C5:
Life in the Slow Lane

Irrespective of success, titles or wealth, it is the single mistake, the momentary lapse of judgement, that so often goes down in history. Such is the harsh truth of loserdom.

Sir Clive Marles Sinclair is a wonderfully wealthy, staggeringly successful and inordinately innovative British inventor and entrepreneur. He was the inventor of the world's first slim-line electronic pocket calculator, the 1972 Sinclair Executive. He also saw the potential for personal computers before almost everyone except Bill Gates, inventing the ZX80, Britain's first mass market computer, which sold for under £100 in the late 1970s.

The son and grandson of engineers, Sinclair showed promise in the same vein from a very early age. As a young boy he designed a submarine. While still at school he wrote for the riveting-sounding magazine *Practical Wireless*. And rather than going to university, he started a mail-order business selling miniature electronics kits he had invented for hobbyists. He also wrote numerous electronics handbooks, and in 1961 started his own business, Sinclair Radionics. Meanwhile, to make ends meet, he was assistant editor on the even more riveting-sounding magazine *Instrument Practice*.

In 1980 Sinclair struck gold when he launched the ZX80 at £79.95 in kit form or £99.95 ready-built. Within two years, his company Sinclair Research was amaking an annual profit of more than eight million pounds.

217

If he had stuck to computers we would probably be remembering him as the British Bill Gates. Alas, he didn't.

Sinclair had always had an weakness for electrically powered vehicles and in 1983, the year he received his knighthood, he set up a research and development company – Sinclair Vehicles Ltd. He invested £8.6m of his own money, raised by selling his shares in Sinclair Research, and entered into a partnership with sports car manufacturer Lotus (what on earth were they thinking?) to develop a battery-operated vehicle. The result was the Sinclair C5, launched in January 1985. It was manufactured by Hoover Ltd at Merthyr Tydfil, spawning the urban myth that the C5 was powered by washing machine motors. In essence it was a tricycle, steered by handles on each side of the driver's seat. No driving licence was required because its top speed was just fifteen miles an hour, and at £399, it was relatively cheap.

In spite of massive publicity, and the support of none other than British Formula One hero Stirling Moss (what on earth was *he* thinking?) the Sinclair C5 was a huge commercial flop. A mere 17,000 were sold.

The truth was that the Sinclair C5 was fatally impractical. Cold weather, not unusual in the British Isles, not only diminished the driver's enjoyment; it dramatically shortened battery life. Moreover, the driver's life was under severe and continual threat, the vehicle being so low on the road as to make it all but invisible to all non-C5 drivers. In an effort to address these issues, side screens were introduced, as well as weather protection, an extra battery and a reflector on a long pole to let other traffic know it was there.

Even after these improvements, the vehicle still suffered from major design flaws, such as a lack of gears and the inability to climb a hill without overheating. Not to mention the biggest problem of all – the Sinclair C5 was irredeemably naff.

Sinclair Vehicles died of embarrassment and went into receivership in October 1985.

OTHER BEST-FORGOTTEN
BRITISH MOTORS

Amphicar

Launched in 1961, the Amphicar, a blend of German and British engineering, was an amphibious car that used Triumph Herald mechanical components. Driven by its rear wheels on land and twin propellers in water, with the front wheels serving as a not altogether satisfactory rudder, it was capable of about 5mph on calm water. If there was the merest hint of a suspicion of a ripple on the water, the Amphicar tended to go backwards. Only 3,878 were ever manufactured, and it sank without trace in 1968.

Morris Marina

Why did so many British cars of the sixties and seventies leak? Rain is not unknown in these isles, so they might at least have got the keeping-the-water-out part right, if nothing else. Made cheaply for the mass market, the 'skip on wheels' was found in a 2006 *Auto Express* survey to be the most scrapped car of the past thirty years.

Mini Moke

The British army asked British Leyland for a light vehicle. The Mini Moke was their response, and the army's was: 'Get lost!'

Triumph TR7

In 1974, as British Leyland combusted in the nightmare of 1970s industrial Britain, they launched the TR7. The vehicle was nothing if not consistent, for there was no part of it that was not rubbish – build quality, controls, electrics and visibility. Far from being a Triumph, it contributed largely to the company's extinction at the end of that troubled decade.

Austin Allegro

What do you get if you combine petrol rationing, a three-day week and power cuts with rampant inflation and repeated strikes in every area of British industry from bread-making to shipbuilding? Probably the Austin Allegro, or 'All Aggro' as it was not-so-fondly known. It had a square steering wheel, branded a 'Quartic logical steering device', which British Leyland believed looked 'advanced' (though some suspected that it had been designed this way because insufficient room had been allowed between the driver's legs and the base of the steering wheel). Nevertheless, the Allegro was adopted by the police, who replaced the steering wheel with a normal one. Despite the fact that it leaked like a … well, a 1970s British car, it somehow survived for ten years.

'*What did the Morris Marina compete against? Walking? The bus?*'

JEREMY CLARKSON

5

Tim Henman:
National Treasure at last

Is Tim Henman a loser? The question has been exercising the nation's best minds for over a decade, ever since he made our hearts skip a beat by reaching the semi-finals at Wimbledon for the first time in 1998.

Perhaps a game of tennis would settle it once and for all.

PLAY!

Henman is a pleasant chap, and was generally realistic about his abilities and the inflated expectations the British public had about him.

WINNER: 15   LOSER: 0

He lost in the Wimbledon semi-final four times, including, in 2001, to the near geriatric Goran Ivanišević. At the time Ivanišević had been injured for two years, was ranked 125 in the world and had only been able to enter the tournament on a wildcard. Tiger Tim came within a few points of victory but, his rhythm messed up by a Great British rain-break, he blew it and found himself picking at his strings in his customarily rueful manner. Ivanišević went on to complete one of Wimbledon's greatest triumphs.

Henman did win lots of tournaments, including ten ATP Masters Series titles.

WINNER: 30   LOSER: 15

Only the second-stringers play those tournaments. Who now remembers Rainer Schuttler, beaten by Henman in the final in Qatar in 1999?

And, at the risk of repeating myself, he did lose in the Wimbledon semi-final four times.

WINNER: 30   LOSER: 30

Henman won more than £10 million in prize money and at least twice that in endorsements and sponsorships.

WINNER: 40   LOSER: 30

That's peanuts compared to, say, Anna Kournikova. Though Kournikova did have an unfair advantage – or two.

And, er, he did lose in the Wimbledon semi-final four times.

DEUCE

The fans: Henman Hill, the passion, the painted faces, the funny hats…

ADVANTAGE: WINNER

The fans: the posh Home Counties girls with big hair, ridiculous hats and painted faces braying 'Come on Tim!'…

He has an attractive and intelligent wife.

ADVANTAGE: WINNER

He never won Wimbledon, choosing instead to lose in the semi-final four times.

RAIN STOPPED PLAY

'A traditional fixture at Wimbledon is the way the BBC TV commentary box fills up with British players eliminated in the early rounds.'

CLIVE JAMES IN *THE OBSERVER, 1981*

4

Everyone Who Has Ever Had a Christmas Number Two

Ever since Dickie Valentine's grotesquely saccharine *Christmas Alphabet* of 1955, the Christmas Number One has been the Holy Grail of the poptastic world.

Christmas Alphabet's special 'festive' qualities ('C is for the candy trimmed around the Christmas tree; H is for the happiness with all the family...') have sent many a listener who has overindulged at Christmas dinner running for the sickbag. Yet they are shared by many other Christmas Number Ones – Jimmy Osmond and the St. Winifred's School Choir, take a bow...

More surprising, perhaps, is how many hardy Christmas perennials have failed to hit the jackpot, including Wham!'s *Last Christmas*, Greg Lake's *I Believe In Father Christmas* and the immortal *Fairytale of New York*, sung by Shane McGowan and Kirsty MacColl, which was held to second place by the Pet Shop Boys' cover of *Always on my Mind*. McGowan was moved to complain that his song had been beaten to the top spot by 'two queens and a drum machine.'

The Beatles sat at Number Two with *She Loves You* at Christmas 1963, but they had little cause for complaint. For one thing it had already been Number One, and for another the top spot was occupied by their very own *I Want to Hold Your Hand*. They repeated the feat at Christmas 1967 with *Hello, Goodbye* and the *Magical Mystery Tour* EP.

The doyen of the Christmas record, of course, is Sir Cliff Richard, with two Christmas Number Ones to his name, and no fewer than five Number Twos.

From 2004 until 2008, the winner of *The X-Factor* took the top Christmas slot with such tedious certainty that many bookmakers began to accept bets only on the losing second place.

However, in 2009 people power, in the form of a concerted and highly publicized Facebook campaign, gave agit-rocking nu-metallers Rage Against the Machine the most unlikely Christmas Number One in history. Their expletive-laden *Killing in the Name* consigned *X-Factor* winner Joe McElderry's turgid *The Climb* to the ignominy of second place in the festive countdown.

In 2010 the status quo was resumed, with *When We Collide* by *X-Factor's* Matt Cardle winning the prized top spot.

Clive Anderson (interviewing the Bee Gees on his chat show); 'You're hit writers aren't you? I think that's the word anyway.'
Barry Gibb: 'That's the nice word.'
Clive Anderson: 'We're one letter short.'

CHRISTMAS NUMBER TWOS

1952   Jo Stafford *You Belong To Me*

1953   David Whitfield *Answer Me*

1954   David Whitfield *Santo Natale*

1955   Bill Haley & His Comets *Rock Around The Clock*

1956   Frankie Vaughan *The Green Door*

1957   Johnny Otis & His Orchestra With Marie Adams
        Ma He's Making Eyes At Me

1958   Lord Rockingham's XI *Hoots Mon*

1959   Adam Faith *What Do You Want?*

1960   Cliff Richard *I Love You*

1961   Frankie Vaughan *Tower of Strength*

1962   Cliff Richard *The Next Time / Bachelor Boy*

1963   The Beatles *She Loves You*

1964   Petula Clark *Downtown*

1965   Cliff Richard *Wind Me Up (Let Me Go)*

1966   The Seekers *Morningtown Ride*

1967   The Beatles *Magical Mystery Tour* (EP)

1968   Nina Simone *Ain't Got No, I Got Life*

1969   Kenny Rogers & The First Edition
        Ruby Don't Take Your Love To Town

1970   McGuinness Flint *When I'm Dead And Gone*

1971   T Rex *Jeepster*

1972   Chuck Berry *My Ding-A-Ling*

1973   Gary Glitter *I Love You Love Me Love*

1974   Bachman-Turner Overdrive *You Ain't Seen Nothing Yet*

1975   Greg Lake *I Believe In Father Christmas*

1976   Showaddywaddy *Under The Moon Of Love*

1977   The Brighouse & Rastrick Brass Band *Floral Dance*

1978   The Village People *YMCA*

1979	ABBA *I Have A Dream*
1980	John Lennon *(Just Like) Starting Over*
1981	Cliff Richard *Daddy's Home*
1982	Shakin' Stevens *The Shakin' Stevens EP*
1983	Slade *My Oh My*
1984	Wham! *Last Christmas*
1985	Whitney Houston *Saving All My Love For You*
1986	The Housemartins *Caravan Of Love*
1987	The Pogues featuring Kirsty MacColl *Fairytale Of New York*
1988	Kylie & Jason *Especially For You*
1989	Jive Bunny & The Mastermixers *Let's Party*
1990	Vanilla Ice *Ice Ice Baby*
1991	Diana Ross *When You Tell Me That You Love Me*
1992	Michael Jackson *Heal The World*
1993	Take That *Babe*
1994	Mariah Carey *All I Want For Christmas Is You*
1995	Mike Flowers Pops *Wonderwall*
1996	Dunblane *Knockin' On Heaven's Door*
1997	Teletubbies *Teletubbies Say Eh-Oh!*
1998	Chef *Chocolate Salty Balls (PS I Love You)*
1999	Cliff Richard *The Millennium Prayer*
2000	Westlife *What Makes A Man*
2001	Gordon Haskell *How Wonderful You Are*
2002	One True Voice *Sacred Trust*
2003	The Darkness *Christmas Time (Don't Let the Bells End)*
2004	Ronan Keating featuring Yusuf Islam *Father and Son*
2005	Nizlopi *JCB Song*
2006	Take That *Patience*
2007	Katie Melua & Eva Cassidy *What A Wonderful World*
2008	Jeff Buckley *Hallelujah*
2009	Joe McElderry *The Climb*
2010	Rihanna *What's My Name?*

3

Guy Fawkes:
The Only Man Ever to Enter Parliament with Honest Intentions?

In 1604, Guy – or 'Guido' – Fawkes became involved in a plot to assassinate King James I of England (a.k.a. King James VI of Scotland) by blowing up the House of Lords during the following year's State Opening of Parliament. The plotters, led by Robert Catesby, were Catholics who wanted to replace the Protestant James with his nine-year-old daughter, Princess Elizabeth, who would then rule as a Catholic.

Fawkes had already put his money where his mouth was by fighting for a number of years on the continent for Catholic Spain against the Protestant Dutch Republic. He had also attempted to win Spanish support for a Catholic uprising in England, but King Philip II of Spain failed to take the bait, even though at the time Spain was at war with the English.

The 'Gunpowder Plot' was launched on 20 May 1604, at an inn on the Strand. One of the conspirators, Thomas Percy, had gained access to a house owned by the Keeper of the King's Wardrobe, John Whynniard. He was joined there by Fawkes, posing as a servant under the alias of John Johnson. The original plan was to dig a tunnel from Whynniard's house to Parliament, but the pair soon discovered that Whynniard also owned a storeroom handily situated directly beneath the House of Lords. The conspirators purchased the lease to the storeroom, and over the following months stockpiled a total of thirty-six barrels of gunpowder.

The State Opening had initially been scheduled for February 1605, but was postponed several times due to concerns about plague. The date was finally set for Tuesday 5 November.

As the fateful date drew near, Fawkes was chosen to light the fuse. He would then make his escape across the Thames. Meanwhile, a revolt in the Midlands would lead to the capture of Princess Elizabeth, who would be brought south and installed on the throne of England. By that time, Fawkes would be long gone, having fled to the continent.

The plotters' consciences were pricked by the fact that a number of Catholics would attend the State Opening. An anonymous letter was sent to one of them, Lord Monteagle, warning him to stay away. Monteagle showed it to King James, who ordered a search of the cellars beneath Parliament. Fawkes was arrested as he was leaving the cellar in which the gunpowder was found. When asked what he was up to, he gave a frank answer. He informed his captors that had intended 'to blow you Scotch beggars back to your native mountains.'

James ordered that 'John Johnson' be tortured in order to draw from him the names of his fellow conspirators, and he was taken to the Tower of London. Fawkes confessed but steadfastly refused to divulge the names of the others, before finally cracking under great duress.

The trial of the eight conspirators began on Monday 27 January 1606. The verdict was foregone conclusion. All were found guilty of high treason and sentenced to death. They would be dragged backwards to the scaffold by a horse. There they would be hanged, but cut down before they died. Their genitals would then be cut off and burned in front of them. After this their bowels and hearts would be removed, before they were finally decapitated, with their body parts left to be eaten by the birds.

Fawkes was the last to mount the scaffold. The severely weakened man managed to climb high enough up the ladder to ensure that the drop was sufficient to break his neck, so that he did not have to suffer the ensuing agonies – though that did not stop the diligent officials from inflicting the gruesome indignities on his lifeless body.

We commemorate the whole merry occasion every 5 November.

'Vote Guy Fawkes... The Only Man Ever To Enter Parliament With Honest Intentions.'
POSTER PLACED ON THE DOOR OF ONE OF THE HOLYROOD OFFICES OF THE SCOTTISH SOCIALIST PARTY, AS REPORTED IN *THE EVENING TIMES*, 2003

2

Eddie 'the Eagle' Edwards: Jumping to Failure

Before the Calgary Winter Olympics of 1988, Michael 'Eddie' Edwards was a plasterer from Cheltenham. Actually, he still is a plasterer from Cheltenham, but between then and now he has had quite a time.

The basic facts of Eddie's rise to global fame, with appearances on the Johnny Carson Show and his very own entry in the *Oxford Book of Words and Phrases* ('pulling an Eddie') are simple. Edwards had caught the skiing bug on a school holiday aged thirteen, since when he had harboured an ambition to compete for Britain in the Winter Olympics. Not being good enough to get into the highly competitive downhill events, he opted for the scariest alpine sport of them all – ski jumping. In those days, every country could enter one competitor for each sport: Eddie correctly surmised that he would be the only British entrant, and booked his ticket to Calgary.

He was not a natural ski jumper. He weighed in at almost twenty pounds heavier than anyone else in competitive ski jumping. He was also dangerously short-sighted, having to wear thick glasses that tended to mist up as he sped down the slope. Unsurprisingly, he suffered from a lack of sponsorship. The years before Calgary were spent sleeping on friends' floors, farm sheds, and even, on one occasion, in a Finnish mental hospital. His boots were too big, and he had to stuff socks into them to pad them out; his broken ski helmet was held together by string; and without access to proper facilities he was forced to practise at home, by jumping off the wardrobe or chairs onto his bed, in an effort to perfect the explosive take-off required for a successful jump.

When this eccentric Brit arrived in Calgary, ranked 55th in the world, he quickly became a hero to all but the skiing establishment. His fellow participants and the Olympic officials were horrified and embarrassed, but most people admired Eddie's courage and spirit. He even managed to set a British record, when he jumped 73.5 metres (though the winner, the Finn Matti Nykänen, jumped a full 45 metres further). A new rule would make it impossible for rank amateurs to enter Winter Olympic events in the future.

After Calgary Edwards' life entered a brief non-loser phase. Though he had finished 58th in a field of 59 – the 59th jumper broke his leg – he is reputed to have earned £87,000 in the first week after the Olympics. Subsequently, with advertising campaigns, personal appearances and speaking engagements at £10,000 a throw, he amassed around £400,000. He also had a number two hit record in Finland, and reached the top 50 in Britain with another record. Sadly, though, by 1992 Eddie was in the bankruptcy court, and living back home with his parents. His failure to qualify for the 1992, 1994 or 1998 Olympics brought an end to his competitive ski-jumping days.

Still, as Tennyson almost said:

'Better to have jumped and lost
than never to have jumped at all.'

1

Now we can hardly have a winner in a book of losers, can we?

Index of Incompetence